WHAT PEOPLE ARE SAYING ABOUT

RIPENING TIME

Sherry Anderson opened one door when she co-authored *The Feminine Face of God*. Now she opens another. With honesty, wealth of experience, and penetrating questions, she leads us again. The issue, she says, *is not to know the map [of elderhood], but to be the map*. These writings are a rich and important resource for all who wonder how to reach the true harvest of their lives. You will not be disappointed.
Paula D'Arcy, author of *Waking Up To This Day, and Gift of the Red Bird*

This book is a harvest of shining wisdom—earthy, funny, lyrical, and very human. Maturity, Anderson says, is as complex and rich as an old-vine wine. And it is hard work—the fruit of a life lived with honesty, soul, and care for others. Stand by and for what you love, she urges, and the miracle will happen!
Janine Canan, author of *Messages from Amma* and *She Rises Like the Sun*.

Here is the book I've been waiting for—an expression of hard-earned wisdom that reveals aging as a journey of profound transformation.
Rabbi Shefa Gold, Author of *The Magic of Hebrew Chant: Healing the Spirit, Transforming the Mind*, and *Deepening Love*

Anderson explores the questions of maturity with depth, sensitivity, and humor, in a voice that is at once touchingly personal and deeply wise. A must read for anyone over 55.
Roger Housden, author of the best-selling *Ten Poems* series, and in 2014, *Keeping the Faith Without a Religion*.

...Anderson's beautifully written exploration of becoming an elder is a conversation that reverberates inside the reader.
Diane Wolkstein, author, *Inanna, Queen of Heaven and Earth* and *The Magic Orange Tree*.

Ripening Time invites the reader to engage the aging process with an imaginative boldness—challenging the lies we've been told, confronting our fears and offering a compass for the years ahead. This is a book you will want to keep with you as you continue becoming a wise elder.
Nancy Sylvester, President of the *Institute for Communal Contemplation and Dialogue*; former President, *Leadership Council for Women Religious*.

The perfect book for baby boomers (and all who love us) on our next frontier—aging. By sharing her personal quest and the art of inner inquiry, Sherry Anderson guides us outside our mind traps into the possibility of a grace-filled reality.
Jessica Britt, Founding Teacher, *Diamond Approach North Sea (DANS)*, The Netherlands

Luminous, tender and wise, Sherry Anderson's beautiful book encourages us to face what we so often avoid—the inevitability of our own aging. Without sugarcoating the hardships, she leads us into uncharted territory. Through her eyes, we realize that far from dark and dreadful, old age is a stage of life graced with gifts and blessings every bit as abundant as those of youth.
Jalaja Bonheim, author of *Evolving Towards Peace*

What great timing! As women are leaping ahead in assuming leadership roles, Anderson draws on her considerable experience and wisdom to offer a guide to growing wise and big-hearted, along with growing old. She teaches with great stories, leads by gently inviting and encourages with obvious love and care.
David Kundtz, author of *Quiet Mind: One-Minute Retreats from a Busy World*

Ripening
Time

Inside Stories for Aging with Grace

Ripening Time

Inside Stories for Aging with Grace

Sherry Ruth Anderson

CHANGE
MAKERS
BOOKS

Winchester, UK
Washington, USA

First published by Changemakers Books, 2013
Changemakers Books is an imprint of John Hunt Publishing Ltd., Laurel House, Station Approach,
Alresford, Hants, SO24 9JH, UK
office1@jhpbooks.net
www.johnhuntpublishing.com
www.changemakers-books.com

For distributor details and how to order please visit the 'Ordering' section on our website.

Text copyright: Sherry Ruth Anderson 2013

ISBN: 978 1 78099 963 0

Design: Stuart Davies

Cover art by Heather Preston

Printed in the USA by Edwards Brothers Malloy

We operate a distinctive and ethical publishing philosophy in all
areas of our business, from our global network of authors to
production and worldwide distribution.

CONTENTS

Other Titles

Crazy Talk: A Study of the Discourse of Schizophrenic Speakers by Sherry Rochester and J. R. Martin. Plenum Press: New York, 1979.

The Feminine Face of God: The Unfolding of the Sacred in Women by Sherry Ruth Anderson and Patricia Hopkins. Bantam Press: New York, 1991.

The Cultural Creatives: How 50 Million People Are Changing the World. Paul H. Ray, Ph.D. and Sherry Ruth Anderson, Ph.D. Harmony Books: New York, 2000.

A Woman's Descent to the Sacred. 2011. Short Film. Available on http://www.awomansdescenttothesacred.com/watch.html and *www.vimeo.com/25536781*

This book is dedicated
with gratitude to my teachers
Hameed Ali (A.H. Almaas), Jeanne Hay,
and Seung Sahn Soen Sa Nim
and
with blessings to my goddaughters
Catherine Anderson Price and Hallelujah Adar Anderson

I love you, gentlest of Ways,
who ripened us as we wrestled with you.
~Rainer Maria Rilke, Rilke's Book of Hours,
 translated by Joanna Macy and Anita Barrows

Prologue

Is there a Map?

About halfway through what I was calling My Year of Living Dangerously, a year I thought might stretch into permanent retirement with me languishing gloriously on the sofa reading novels and watching the wind shake through the poplars across the street, the matter of growing old came knocking on my door. It wasn't what you might think—some bad news about a fall or the death of a dear friend or discovering overnight that I had developed jowls. It was a call, a wake-up and show-up and pay-attention call that I had not expected.

It happened on a Sunday morning in August as I was rolling up my sweaty yoga mat at the end of class. A tall, blonde woman I knew slightly asked if we could talk for a few minutes. We huddled in the corner as the next class of eager yoginis rushed past us to stake out their territory.

"I'm turning fifty at the end of this year," the woman said. "I heard from some friends that you took them on a trip down the Colorado River in April. They told me you did a powerful ritual about becoming elders. I need that."

Wow, pretty direct, this beautiful woman, I thought. She knows what she wants. We walked outside, and I gave her a couple of ideas for creating an elders circle for her birthday. "Call me if you want any help," I said.

A few weeks later the woman, I'll call her Eve, sent me an email. It was a little stiff, the way emails are between virtual strangers. "You inspired me with your suggestion of how I might mark my fiftieth year and prepare for my entry into 'Cronehood'. I would love to continue the conversation, if you were open to it—this last month has thrown me into some really interesting explorations of how to be in partnership, and yet not lose myself (that age old thing!)."

She invited me to tea, saying that she had an English garden attached to the back of her little houseboat in San Francisco Bay. She included a photo of a small deck covered with pots of red geraniums and white begonias and a profusion of summer flowers I couldn't identify. Beyond her floating garden was the dark green bay and the washed out blue of the summer sky. I was enchanted. What an old-fashioned thing to do—sit in a garden drinking tea, and as Eve put it, continue the conversation.

Two weeks later, after yoga, I was in Eve's houseboat kitchen trying not to smack my head on the sharp angles of her cabinets. She made us a salad of beets and goat cheese and the promised tea. We carried the plates out to her deck where otters were splashing in the water a few yards away and a convoy of white pelicans sailed high above us. We chatted about her family and her life in England and her travels around the world and my work—almost everything, it seemed, except the Cronehood that was supposed to be the point of our getting together. Just as I was wondering how I could politely leave, the conversation took an intimate turn.

Eve confided that she was in a ten-year relationship with a man named Henry to whom she seemed to be giving herself away, and she was getting sick of it. A horribly familiar resentment had set in, which was bad enough, she said, but now something worse was happening, something that really worried her. Her usual cool righteousness was starting to seethe and spurt like an out-of-control volcano. She was sure this was going to destroy her relationship, but she couldn't seem to shove her anger back down, no matter how hard she tried. Did I have any wisdom to offer (from, presumably, the far side of Cronehood where my sixty-five-year-old self was residing)?

I was actually feeling joy. It looked to me like Eve's generations-long maternal family pattern of long-suffering Ice Queens was being melted by lava flows of some upwelling energy. "This is a good thing," I told her. "Something life giving seems to be moving in you, and you need to go with it. Without spilling it all over Henry, of course."

She grinned. Evidently, spilling it all over Henry had a certain appeal.

Then she leaned forward and asked a question I was to hear many times over the next few years. "Is there a map? I need a map for this new territory I'm headed into."

A Map for the Territory

Eve's question stayed with me. We met again for lunch, and then for walks through the hills above her house in Tiburon. Over the next few months, we became friends, hiking through the dry grass of summer as the hills turned into pale wheaty hay and the skies lost their clouds. Once in a while I'd remember how we met and Eve's question and I'd wonder: Is there a map for growing old?

Early one morning in October, I made my way through a dreary line of commuter traffic to meet Eve at a French bistro in a made-over garage. Once we had our coffee (okay, mocha lattes) and the famous croissants and some strawberry preserves that Eve had brought from home, she surprised me by picking up our original conversation as if we'd been discussing nothing else for the past three months.

"There *ought* to be a map," she said, emphasizing the *ought* as if we'd been debating the matter. "Something that comes after *The Feminine Face of God*. When you and your friend Pat wrote that book, you said we were coming into a time of massive changes, of 'spirituality in the fast lane.' Well, that time is here and everybody knows it. Now what?"

She went on, gesturing with the remains of her second croissant, explaining that she didn't mean "now what" in general. She meant it in particular about women like her, women in the middle of their lives.

"When *sacred feminine* no longer sets off shock waves in the culture, and women like me are running things, becoming Secretary of State and Speaker of the House and soon President," she said, "what is the way for us? I want a map for turning fifty and for the territory ahead, sixty and seventy and eighty. And what about my young women clients who come to me for coaching? They're in their thirties and forties and if I'm not moving into my own...what do you call it? Growing edge? Growing up? Growing wise? They'll have no one ahead to show the way. They'll have nothing to move into, and they'll keep looking back to their twenties as their best years." She looked exasperated. "Come on!"

I told Eve I'd think about it and get back to her. As it turned out, I didn't actually *think* about her questions so much as feel jolted by them. Have you ever been startled in that way—as if you're headed to your gate in some foreign airport with all the noise and flight announcements blaring in another language and suddenly you hear your name called on the sound system? And bang, you're right there, feet on the ground and paying attention.

If you've had that kind of wake-up call, then you know the intense effect that Eve's question about a map had for me. It seemed like an assignment that had my name on it. Whether I could find an answer was another matter entirely but I knew I wasn't going turn away.

A Longing for Elders

What happened next was that I started to feel lonely for a woman named Esse Chaisin whom I hadn't seen in fifteen years. It had taken a long time to find her in the first place—one of the very few women teaching Kaballah in the United States at the end of the twentieth century. At the time I located Esse, she was seventy years old, a respected elder, and I was eager to interview her for my book on women's spiritual development.

When she agreed, I caught the train from Manhattan to Long

Island for what turned out to be an exhausting ride. What made it so tiring was the bustling crowd of shtetl characters in my mind, as my family's (modern, conservative Jewish) ideas about traditional Jews joined my own bleak imagination to produce a sour-pussed old woman shrouded in black, crowned with a plastic-looking sheitel, the traditional wig. I was sure she'd hear about one word of my ridiculous questions and throw me out.

"Hi," she said, when the taxi dropped me at her bungalow. "Come on in." I stared. She was wearing a form-fitting fuschia sweater and skirt outfit, and her gorgeous white hair was clearly her own. Moreover, Esse turned out to adore questions. Over the next few hours, she allowed me to ask penetrating questions about her life. The more confronting I was, the more she enjoyed it. She had always liked questions, she told me, but in her forties, she developed a passion for them.

"Bring them on," she challenged, laughing. "They open me deeper to my truth, and through the truth, to Ha Shem, the Holy One."

"I've never met anyone like you in my life," I blurted out. "How did you get to be so fearless?"

From her teacher, she said, Madam Irmis Popoff. Trained by G. I. Gurdijieff, the founder of a spiritual school called The Fourth Way, the fierce Madam Popoff was a master of self-observation. "She taught me to bring my attention right to the present moment so I could shake myself from the waking sleep most of us walk around in, from daydreaming and absentmindedness," Esse told me. "And she showed me the power of penetrating questions so I could know myself."

And then one day without warning, after eight years of working together, Madam Popoff ended their relationship. "It's time to go," she announced. "If you've learned what I've taught you, you'll be fine. If not, not. Either way, it's up to you now."

And that was that. Esse's time as a student was over. She was on her own.

Remembering the story made me sad. I missed Esse. I wished I could talk to her about this elders thing. I wanted to ask her about the map for growing old and wise. So I Googled her. To my delight, I could track her life through years of teaching courses at a synagogue in Brooklyn. The listings continued for a while and then stopped. I kept Googling until I found a later reference in a book written by one of Esse's students. It was a dedication that began "For Esse Chaisin, of Blessed Memory."

Hot tears rushed to my eyes. Although we hadn't spoken often after our meeting on Long Island, Esse had been a placeholder for me, an elder. One of the many. I realized that the women I had interviewed while writing my book had become my own circle of wise women. Their life stories flashed in my memory often, showing up my blind spots, revealing my stubborn opinions, inspiring my courage. And even more than their stories, I carried the felt sense of their presence. Each woman was unique and every one, in her own way, was faithful to the truth that was unfolding through her. I depended on them for some ballast, some ground of connection to a feminine wisdom that was genuine and powerful.

But by the time I turned sixty-five, I knew I'd been hiding behind those women. Their wisdom came so easily to my lips, I hadn't bothered to listen for my own. Esse was gone, along with many others from that circle. My elders were leaving as surely— more surely—than Madame Popoff parted from Esse. I'd been dozing, feeling safe back in the second tier. Now, abruptly, I got the message. It's our turn now. My generation's turn—whether we're ready or not. An abrupt but definite invitation: the elders are leaving—will you step up?

And then there was that other invitation—Eve's voice demanding: Is there a map?

A Feeling For The Territory

I got back to Eve and asked her to tea in my backyard under the redwoods. It was a little cold to be outside and the neighbor's dog was whining, but we sat out anyway to catch the last sunlight before the November rains.

"I'm no map maker," I told her right away, wanting to get things straight. "I'm traveling through unknown territory myself. The only thing I have is a kind of compass."

"That will do," she said, and wanted to hear about the compass. "It's questions," I said. "I know how to listen for the questions, to wait for them to come to me."

I can't remember if she just stared at me, but I know I felt the need to add, "Soul-level questions."

"That's what we need now," she shot back. "Help for living into the questions. You've got a feeling for the territory. That's what I want—not one more bloody list of the seven routes to excellence, the five rules for mastery, the hierarchies and nested sets and branching trees that treat my life like it's a problem to be solved, as if I'm some little widget in a monopoly game that has to be set on the right lines or I'll end up in jail!"

She was turning red. The lava flows that had been melting her Ice Queen demeanor all these months were moving fast now and seemed to be headed straight at me. Get going, she was saying. Start telling whatever truth you know how to tell about growing old. It's time.

A New Time

What kind of time *is* this when the ones who are coming up behind us want maps and we don't have any? Or, to be honest, we have a superabundance of maps and soothsayers and doomsayers and fearless prophets. We just don't have anything that we trust to show the way into...what?

A new time.

What does *that* mean?

What if we had more time? What if, instead of dying in child-birth in our thirties or wearing down by forty or forty-five like so

7

many of our ancestors, we had an extra thirty years of life, an extra generation and then some to grow into our human possibility? What could we become?

For most of human history, it's as if we have had long springtimes and only the briefest of summers, a lot of time to put down roots and sprout but almost none to mature. But now, around the world and especially in the developed countries, more people are living longer, healthier lives than ever before. Our normal life span, which stayed at an almost steady twenty years for most of human history, has leapt in an evolutionary eyeblink to seventy-eight years in the West.

Why is this so important? Think about how helpless we are as infants and children compared to other species. It takes us so long to be able to live without our parents' support, so very long to develop our intelligence and adaptability and skills, to grow in our capacity for compassion and wisdom, good judgment, and discernment. To put it bluntly, it takes all of us a frightfully long time to grow up and many of us never do.

So is it any wonder that my friend Eve was asking for a map and I didn't have one to hand her? The sudden spurt in longevity over the last fifty years has changed the landscape for growing old. As one expert put it: "If you don't yet know how to navigate your way through the new old age, join the club."[1]

On the other hand, our growing season has almost doubled. Doesn't that make you wonder what these years are for? That's precisely what I've been wondering for the past twenty years: How do I make the time ahead count? How can my generation and the ones coming after us not just fritter our later years away, not doze through our aging as if it were not a matter of great human consequence?

As I'm about to turn seventy, I can see how young I was when I first started to ask those questions. What I scarcely considered was that genuine maturity is a development, an organic process that has its own good timing. It didn't matter that the Jungian analyst Marion Woodman tried to counsel me. "If I knock and a door opens, I walk through," she said. "If it doesn't open, it's not my door." I couldn't imagine living that way. I couldn't imagine that anything worthwhile could come without my storming gates—whatever gates stood in the way of growing up and growing wise.

But I knew that I couldn't find my way alone. In the early 1990s I started looking for circles of elders where it was possible to speak honestly about the inner experience of growing old. I imagine that there had to have been such circles, but I couldn't find any. So I began to create them— places and occasions where my friends over fifty, and then others I didn't know, could gather together and delve into the deep matters of aging.

Over time, we learned how to invite and welcome the intimate questions that elders almost never say out loud. We met in seminar rooms and retreat centers and inquiry groups in people's homes. Some of these explorations lasted for a year, others for just week or a day. By 2012, the gatherings included teleconferences across Alaska and between the two coasts of the United States. What has mattered most, I think, are the ways we have learned to listen to each other and to ourselves, allowing time for our questions to develop into genuine inquiries. Or maybe I have it backwards and the deep listening is a doorway to something else. Delving into the questions, following the thread of our truth can free us from crusty, old ideas we've carried from childhood and from our culture about who we are and how we have to be. With this freedom, so much is possible: the way our hearts open; the way we are caught by surprise at the pure value of being here, just as we are now; the grace of this time of our lives.

In the pages that follow, I tell stories from these years of sharing the great and powerful questions that life brings us as we age. I am indebted to the teachings of the Kwan Un Zen School where I was a student and later a senior teacher in the 1970s and

80s, and to the Diamond Approach to Spiritual Development® where I have been studying and teaching for over two decades. And since discoveries are best made personally and directly, I've provided some inquiries at the end of this book, along with a guide for working alone and also with friends, should you wish to explore further.

For every question I've raised, you will find many more of your own. For every story I tell, your own stories will take you further. I hope you will find in these pages not so much a map but a compass for exploring your own experiences of aging; and I hope you will discover the grace that unfolds as a blessing and a joy as you come to trust and follow your own deep questions.

PART I

TIME TO RIPEN

The question we encounter as we grow old is this:
How do we allow ourselves to be shaped and transformed by our
experience?
Allow it to ripen us if it will?
Jim Thomas, San Francisco, 2011

Chapter 1

A Season of Ripening

When a growing season is long enough for fruits to mature, we can call it a season of ripening. Our species has entered this season now—a time when we have a never before chance to grow up beyond what most of us have barely imagined. Have you thought about this? Dreamed into it for yourself or for our common good, for the pure wisdom and lovingkindness that might develop in our world? And if you wonder about what is possible for us now, do you want to pursue the possibilities? To delve into the deep questions this ripening season opens?

Personally, I find it a great relief to dump the usual, politically correct, words for aging—elderhood, senior citizens, golden agers—and all the horrid ones I won't even bother with here—to consider the possibilities of ripening. Those other words are so stale, used up, and misused that they trap my imagination in a thousand musty certainties. So I started searching around for something fresh and finally found *ripening*. It's from the Old English *reopan*, dating back ten centuries to the root verb *to reap*. It lets us reframe the perspective about growing old to ask: What can we reap from a long life if we are conscious, if we pay attention, if we care?

My big Webster's that sits on its own table next to the computer reads like a guidebook to the possibilities of the ripening season. To ripen is to be *fully grown and developed, as in ripe fruit and ripe wheat*, it says. And also: *having mature knowledge, understanding or judgment*. And a third meaning: *of advanced years, as in a ripe old age*. And my favorite: (a) *brought by aging to full flavor or the best state, mellow*; and (b) *smelly, stinking, as in ripe cheese*.

This sums it up pretty well, don't you think? The promise—to come to our full flavor as human beings, to mature into the best possibilities of our nature. And the reality—the full flavor of living a long life isn't just mellow. It's also smelly, stinking. Growing old is an adventure, but it's no stroll through the rose garden, no "grow old along with me, the best is yet to be." Whoever believes that is living in Disneyland. To ripen—not just grow up but to keep on maturing through our entire lives—takes great courage and great vulnerability. And I guess I'd have to add, a huge dollop of grace. We can end up unripe, bitter, not able to reap the fruits of this life because overwhelming circumstances make us lose hope, or because we get tangled in our culture's stories and lies about aging. Or maybe we end up losing hope because dementia—our parents' or our partner's or our own—in one of its many dreadful forms throws a pall over all the possibilities, shutting off our curiosity and spirit for living into the truth of our life as it is unfolding.

There are no guarantees. Yet there's the likelihood for us, as there is for all of life, that we can fully mature if our possibilities are nurtured and cultivated. Ripening, in other words, is natural. We should expect it. And also, we should look with a skeptical eye on the odd but common assumption that all our growth is over by, say, thirty. I hereby throw down the gauntlet against that careless assumption. I propose that, since we do not know what reaches and dimensions of our humanity are possible as we age, we engage the question. All the questions—whatever we can discover about how we can grow old consciously. We already know too much about what diminishes—hearing, eyesight, short-term memory, speed of recall and calculation, and so on. That is not so interesting. But to consider what grows, what develops, what ripens—that, I propose, is interesting indeed!

The Question

I was feeling rather pleased with myself for finding a word like *ripening*. And then I spent the afternoon with my friend Jim

Thomas, a white-haired Texan whom I consider to be a wise elder.

"You know," Jim said, "I think as we grow old, we're like fruit on wild trees. A lot of us stay small and hard, relatively untouched by all our years of experience, while others ripen into fullness."

I told him about an apple tree that grew in the vacant lot around the corner from my childhood home in Atlantic City. Starting in April I'd wander over every week or two to watch its pale buds blossom into frothy white flowers and then disappear for a whole month—gone!—before tiny green apples appeared. All through the summer I'd visit the tree, waiting for the apples to turn yellow so I could take a few experimental bites. But I never could eat those apples. They stayed bitter. By late October, moldy anyway, they were blown to the ground by the hard, ocean winds.

I was getting depressed remembering the apples. All that growing and in the end, crashing to the earth and rotting. Well, really, what's the point of it all?

Instead of joining my gloomy contemplations, Jim lobbed a question. "Exactly. How can we let ourselves be shaped and transformed by our experience? How do we let life ripen us if it will?"

What's Possible

When we talk about human accomplishments, we almost never include maturing. What interests us, in our post-modern conversations, are the heights of attainment—the best athletes, the most brilliant inventions, the greatest works of art. In more rarefied settings, we concern ourselves with the profound reaches of consciousness—a realization of unity, emptiness of self, or qualities of great compassion and wisdom.

But the question about maturity is different. It asks what is possible for all of us, for people who live a full measure of years.

Before life extends to its full measure, we can only guess about its fruition. But with a long life, we have a chance to find out what we can be—to ripen into our full human development.

And we can discover another sense of ripening, too: the taste and richness of our full, juicy humanity. When I think of this kind of ripeness, certain elders come immediately to mind. I imagine it might be the same with you, if you recollect your own elders. My elders aren't paragons of perfection; they can be grouchy, sad, and frightened at times, and they can also be people of no age. What inspires me is their undivided humanness—how they are willing to be present to all that life brings—sorrow, grief, joy, emptiness, lostness, celebration, stillness—and let it deepen and transform them again and again. They make me want to live like that—wholehearted—into the breadth and length of my years.

Not all people can digest the experiences that life brings. But in this era of history, more and more of us have a chance to do so. The door is open. Invitations are arriving every day. Elders we've relied on are dying or already gone, leaving open their places in the circle. Those younger are demanding maps, asking us to share whatever truth we have to tell. If we are willing, if we have the heart to step forward, the ones who have walked before us and the ones who are coming after us are calling:

Will you, won't you, will you, won't you, will you join the dance?
Will you, won't you, will you, won't you, won't you join the dance?[2]

So the invitation is waiting. We can either reach out and take it or turn away. I'm going to take it and I hope you will too. I don't have the map that Eve was looking for, but I can offer a compass for the soul-deep questions. I've learned a lot from my students and friends and will bring in their experiences as well. If your eye has a glint of curiosity and your heart longs to live the truth that's unfolding now, come and join the dance. Our first step will be a confrontation with one of the biggest lies our culture tells—that old age is boring!

Chapter 2

Old Age is Boring

Why aren't all of us who are over about fifty-five intrigued by what it is like to be maturing now? I don't mean complaining or comparing notes on the best doctors or massage therapists or vitamin supplements. I mean why aren't we diving in, paying rapt attention to the depth levels of our experience?

As I ask the question, I think I know the answer. Or at least I know the first part of the answer, the first obstacle that arises to exploring the territory where ripening is possible but not guaranteed. As I began this book and very often throughout the writing, I would be interrupted by the arrival of a bossy inner commentator. *Old age is boring,* my would-be advisor would announce. *Boring! What is the matter with you anyway? Get rid of this ridiculous preoccupation you've developed with getting old and find something you can be passionate about. What about hang gliding? Mountain biking? Tango?*

My inner advisor is convinced it has the lowdown on old age. And although I hear it personally, I'm sure it is not mine alone. Its convictions are honed by our culture, supported by our friends, nurtured by memories so early they feel like the fuzzy blankets we clung to as children. Its viewpoint provides the blinders that come down just when we are starting to get real. It's the guardian at the gates that keeps us from entering the mysteries within, the chief lie that smothers our curiosity about what is possible for us now.

I have learned the power of this lie all too well in delving into the experience of growing old. Whenever I have neared an edge where fear lies or grief waits or where I stand mute or empty, the voice of this lie implores me to hurry on—not to enter the other country, explore the different game. So this, I think, is where graceful aging needs to begin. The marker at the trailhead reads: *Old Age is Boring.*

When Does it Start?

I wonder when it begins to take root in our psyches, this notion of old age being something dull? I can't remember thinking this way as a child. But by high school, I was a full-grown believer. My father's parents, Lena and Max, lived a few blocks from my school, and I was supposed to visit them whenever I could. My father would say, in a fake casual way but I knew it meant a lot to him, "Just drop in and say hi."

I found every excuse not to go. When I finally did show up at their apartment on Pacific Avenue, the TV was on and my grandparents were sitting next to each other on the sofa, watching Liberace or Groucho Marx in the middle of the afternoon. Though their place was stuffed with furniture, I could almost smell the emptiness—dry as old dust left behind in cracks you couldn't see. It made me want to run out of there as fast as I could and never come back.

But my grandparents would be so glad to see me. My grandmother would hurry to the kitchen to bring me a glass of milk and the hard little *hamantashen* she kept in a box on top of the refrigerator for the grandchildren. My grandfather would kiss me and rub his bristly mustache over my cheek, making me giggle. I should come here more often, I'd think guiltily. It makes them so happy. But in the depths of my teenaged self, I would rant: *Getting old is boring, hideously boring!* And I stayed away from the little apartment with the blaring television for months at a time.

When I began writing this book, I was as old as my grandparents were then. Memories of them began coming up almost immediately, shadowy poignancies that tugged at my heart. But I did not welcome them. Instead I found myself bored. I'm tired of writing about getting old, I thought, barely months into the process. Whatever made me think that this was a grand adventure, a new country to be discovered? There is so much else to do in my life right now.

This Aging Thing

You know how it is when you don't want to look at something that's disturbing you and it shows up everywhere—you hear a song on the radio or get an email or catch sight of a passing bumper sticker? One bright October day, around the time I first started getting tangled up in how boring the whole topic of aging was, I took a walk through a marsh with my friend Harry. We had stopped to admire two feet of a shining grass snake wriggling into the weeds when, pretty much out of nowhere, Harry said, "Honestly, I can't see why you're spending your time on this aging thing."

I squinted up at him. He's got ice blue eyes that make women take a second look and then a third. "I just don't think aging is interesting for people like us," he said. What kind of people is that, I wondered. I once saw a photo of Harry when he was in his thirties and still had hair and was drop dead gorgeous. Maybe "people like us" meant beautiful people, but I didn't think I'd make the cut.

"I'll be turning sixty-five in two months," he said, "and I'm not really different than I was in my thirties. I'm the same weight I've always been."

He went on to tell me how he's as much in love with life now as when he was twenty-one. He'd walk to Trafalgar Square to eat his lunch outside, he said, and watch for moments of beauty. He'd been reading Stendhal and fallen into a full-bore enthrallment that hasn't let up. "I'm still searching the world for moments of beauty," he said, "like just now, when an iridescence of grass snake comes into our lives." He paused, gazing into the tall weeds where the snake had disappeared.

I couldn't think of anything to say. I was still wondering what "people like us" meant. We stood there for a while and when I started to walk on, Harry stopped me. "Age has nothing to do with it, you see. Nothing at all," he said, flashing those exotic eyes.

Why was I struck so dumb at Harry's question about spending time on this aging thing? Probably, as I think about it now, it was because I was so pleased to be included as someone ready for moments of beauty, not to mention being as fit and healthy as I was in my twenties (not true, but never mind). And because maybe, although Harry didn't mention this explicitly, he was implying that I was a bit fascinating and exotic like himself. Yes, I could see how I might be included in that lively, fortunate, ageless membership. Certainly, I could not think of a single good reason to dispute it.

Later, I could. Many answers came to me, the kind I elaborate in the chapters ahead. But the powerful, first answer, was this: *Swallowing the lies of our cultural assumptions means that I can't digest anything else.*

I don't know for sure if lies about growing old are poisoning our future but they might be. Here's something I do know: naming the lies smokes them out.

Naming The Lies

About six months after my walk with Harry, I had a chance to watch some of the lies about growing old go up in flames. I flew to Alabama, to a world about as foreign to my San Francisco Bay liberal self as Marrakesh, for a conference called "Womenspeak." Close to a thousand women gathered in the Mobile Convention Center, women from Bible study groups across the South, African Americans and whites, young and old and in-between. About half were on scholarship from homeless shelters and halfway houses, and others were working class and middle class, so far as I could tell.

On the main day of the conference, workshops were scheduled in the morning and again in the afternoon. I was leading two of them, called, *Birthing the New Elders*. A couple of hundred women showed up. I started by naming the kinds of invitations that prompt women to want to become true elders: the invitations from our own dreams and longings to grow into wisdom; the invitations from younger women for maps of the territory ahead; and the openings left as our own elders die.

"It's our turn now," I said. Then I pulled the mike out of the stand, and strode up the aisle to the back row. Reading the name card on a slim, black woman sitting alone, I said, "Mary Ellen..."

She grinned so I figured it was okay to go on. "Tell me a lie about growing old."

"You get weak and stupid," she shot back.

I crossed the aisle to lean the mike to a large woman with perfectly white hair. "Tell me a lie about getting old."

She waved her arm grandly: "Your children and grand-children will surround you constantly with loving attention in all the ways you've always wanted."

The women were laughing now, and I kept going with the talk show routine. Staying with the question, thrusting the mike toward Lottie and Sister Katherine and Trish and Alice and Anna Mae and countless others, I found they hadn't the least bit of trouble naming the lies. Sometimes their words were greeted with ripples of laughter, and other times there were sighs and head shaking. After awhile the women stopped waiting for the mike and just stood up and shouted out their answers.

When it seemed like we'd dug into the hard-packed soil of old memories, stale ideas, and fond wishes about growing old, when the Catholic Sister from New Jersey and the school teacher from Baton Rouge and the minister from Chapel Hill and the psychol-ogist from Oklahoma City and moms and grandmothers and daughters-in-law from Houston and Lubbock and Atlanta and towns I'd never heard of had tossed in their contributions, it was time to go deeper.

I told them how one Sunday morning I was lying in bed with

my husband Paul, listening to the rain beating hard against the windows and snuggling into his chest. And how he looked at me fondly and said, "Sweetie, when you smile at me like that, you look so young and beautiful."

The women began giggling before I could even get to the part where I was feeling really good about the compliment, basking in it, until it slowly occurred to me to ask, "How do I look when I'm not smiling?"

And my beloved Paul paused for a while, considering. "Old," he told me. "You look old."

The women roared with laughter, rocking back and forth, patting each other on the back, and shaking their heads. Oh yes, they were saying, let's tell it like it is. After awhile I asked them to gather into small circles and one by one, tell each other the truth about how it feels to be the age they are now.

These women didn't have any trouble being interested in the aging thing. They were hungry, even starving, to tear the cultural and personal wrappings off that thing and get to what is real. They were as passionate and on fire and caught in the adventure of living as any people I've ever known. I knew then what group I wanted to be a member of. I want to be counted among the fierce ones who intend to live from the truth of what we are now and what we are becoming.

People like us are definitely interested in this aging thing.

PART II

CLEARING OBSTACLES

In Part I, when I wanted to understand why my curiosity was shutting down, what popped up was: *Old Age is Boring.* I didn't try to talk myself out of it ("Oh come on now, you know how important this is. Can't you just pay attention, etc.") Instead, *boring* turned out to be really interesting, because if you dig a little deeper, you hit a thick shale of cultural beliefs and stories—lies. Once we get a chance to name those lies—especially in the presence of other elders—pow! We turn into fireballs. We laugh at the lies and go for the truth that is underneath them.

I guess you've noticed that my way of digging into a question is not what you might expect. I go for the obstacles first, for whatever is in the way. Because if you discover how an obstacle in consciousness gets its strength, it reveals its secrets to you.

Carl Jung, that great excavator of the depth realms, gives us an overview of where we go from here: *We cannot live the afternoon of life according to the program of life's morning; for what was great in the morning will be little at evening, and what in the morning was true will at evening have become a lie.*[2]

In other words, to live the truth that is ours to live, we need to find out what nurtures that truth and what starves it; to release the morning's reality to live the truth that is unfolding now. We'll begin, as you might expect, with the obstacles. The first is our view of death. The next is our edifice of concepts about growing old.

Chapter 3

We Are Already Naked

We can't talk about ripening without including death, not honestly anyway. Once we pass sixty, we join the ones who know this. Steve Jobs knew it at fifty-one, on the morning he was given a terminal diagnosis for pancreatic cancer. At the end of that day, his doctors took the death sentence back. They said he could count on about thirty more years of life. He turned out to have only seven. I don't think he believed them anyway, because whatever he went through that day seems to have torn away his cloak of invulnerability. I imagine that's how the following year, he could have said to thousands of twenty-somethings at the Stanford commencement ceremony: "You are already naked… There is no reason not to follow your heart."

The speech went viral because Jobs told the truth that people almost never say to twenty-year-olds, the truth all of us over sixty know more or less intimately. Even without a terminal diagnosis, we know that we can count, or almost count, the years we have left on our fingers and maybe our toes. (Do you do this? I do. Usually in bed at night if something has rattled me, I count on my fingers and a few toes the years I think are left for Paul and me. It's a secret communing with a place in my soul that is keeping track.)

All of what we can say about aging, all of what we think, feel, imagine about it—the surprises; the fears, fond hopes, and lies we drink in from our culture; the actual diminishing of strength, resilience, beauty, and memory that we thought belonged to us and were ours to keep; the unsayable substantial truths; the freedom; what love becomes—all of it—is pinned against our death. Indexed to it. Rooted so securely that, if we turn away from the truth of our death, there's no possibility of ripening.

We've shut down against our destiny. Not against our aging of course— we're not in control of that. Only against knowing, against consciousness itself.

Early people, living close to the Earth's cycles of birth, death, and rebirth, created rituals to honor these cycles as sacred in their own lives and in the life of their tribe. Aboriginal and some native peoples preserve these ceremonies today, including honoring their elders. Elders, they say, are the link between the worlds. Elders walk with death at their shoulder, soon to become ancestors.

What if we didn't avoid death? What if we could bear to see ourselves as we are, as the poet Ellen Bass puts it, "reckless, pinned against time"?[1] Would it soften us, make us want to give away all we have gathered—the sofas and blenders and mutual funds, the cars and iPads and 401k's, the refrigerators? Would it make the clouds of our self-concern less dense, the slice of eternity we occupy more transparent and precious? Or would the very truth of death coming near make us cling like mussels to rocks in a stormy sea?

This is how it is for us now—all of it, slamming shut against our vulnerability and actually letting ourselves feel the reactions and distractions and nearness to our death. Can we let ourselves know this? Do we even want to? And can we let each other in on some or all of our mess of feelings and fullness and not knowing and the mystery of it all? And finally, what do we tell the ones coming up behind us asking so earnestly for maps? Do we even want them to know?

* * *

It's a cool July morning with the Pacific fog sitting plump as a grey hen on the far hills. I love the way the mist hides us here in the flatlands for a while, as if we were in a time out of time. When the sun breaks through around noon, I tap my niece

Catherine's number on my cell phone and let it ring. It's 3 p.m. in Rhode Island. Ava's still at day camp, and the baby might be asleep. No answer. Ten minutes later I try again. Someone picks up and I hear Cat yelling goodbye to someone. Now she's shouting into the phone, "Hi Auntie Sherry! I'm just finishing my Filipino stick-fighting lesson!"

Cat's my god-daughter, my brother Howard's second born. At thirty-four, with two kids, her work as an acupuncturist and a terrific husband, she has a life that seems expressible mainly in exclamation marks. Cat is the child of my heart, the girlfriend-daughter I never had. Our conversations reflect this, generally sluicing through the rush of our lives, washing out the gold along with assorted detritus. But once in a while, the pace slows down. Like now.

"How's Paul?" she asks casually, so casually I know she knows the answer, but I tell her anyway.

"We had to call an ambulance on the weekend." I tell her how we were walking on Deer Island when Paul sat down hard on the ground with a pain in his chest that sent me running home for the car. And how it turned out okay after all. No heart attack. On Tuesday, I tell her, we're going into the city for his third stent surgery. I know I'm using the odd locutions around hospitals that I can't seem to avoid, like "They're going to try and open the right artery again," as if an anonymous "They" composed of all the doctors and nurses and consultants in the big Kaiser hospital on Geary Street in San Francisco are aligning in a communal entity that will help my beloved husband's heart beat steadily again. Cat asks a few acupuncture doctor type questions and then comes back to being my friend. "You must be very worried," she says. "It must be really hard."

Last year was hard, I tell her, when Paul slumped on the bathroom floor at 6 in the morning and eight firemen thundered up the stairs carrying a stretcher and some heavy equipment. My own heart froze then against the fear. As I followed the sirening ambulance to the ER in my car, I talked to myself. Don't have an accident. Remember to breathe. Pay attention. You're okay, you can do this. Like when I was seventeen and the firemen ran down our front stairs with my father on the stretcher looking, like Paul, pale as old flannel and scared.

Paul turned out to have food poisoning that first time, I tell Cat. I brought him home, a little green and chagrined at all the fuss. And the second and third times the ambulance came, it was angina but not an attack. Not deadly. We're getting used to it, I say, going to the hospitals. Our bodies are more vulnerable now.

"Getting old sounds awful," she bursts in furiously. "Awful!"

I stop. She's not my girlfriend. All this talk about doctors and ambulances and getting old and vulnerability is upsetting her. Something inside me sits down, like when you're a kid and you're out of breath from running and you find yourself a curb and just sit down.

Silence opens up when you sit down like this. Stillness comes in, as if all the clocks that have been ticking so frantically suddenly stop. I sit down here, in the gap between the worlds, in the slice of eternity between the world of thirty-year-olds in the midst of diapers and summer camp and building a career and finding time for sex and my world now, the world of Paul and me and our sixty- and seventy- and almost-eighty-year-old friends and colleagues.

It's not awful, I say finally. But I feel helpless, wordless. Getting old is so far from awful that I don't know where to begin. I want to tell this to Cat. I would need a lot of time, I want to tell her, and I'd need you not to be in a hurry. I'd need you not to be 3,000 miles away and minutes from having to pick up your baby and get Ava from camp. Maybe I could tell you if we were walking by the ocean the way we did on the day your grandfather died, and maybe a cloud of monarch butterflies would envelop us as they did then and help us find the fierce, honest words we need to understand each other.

I say only, "Getting old is different from what you think."

"Oh yeah, probably is," she says. "Love you. Let's talk again soon."

Unfolding Possibilities

I don't want Cat to think getting old is awful. I can't bear for her to be afraid of what lies ahead, to be trying, at forty-five or fifty or sixty to be "younger next year." I don't care if she bleaches her teeth or colors her hair or gets Botox or pearlescence or whatever the face treatments will be called by then. That's not what's important. I want her to know what growing old is like on the inside.

What if I say, "Getting old is an adventure so exquisite that it breaks me open every single day"? What will she think of when I say "adventure"? When I lived on the side of an active volcano in Ecuador and hiked into the rain forest and hurtled through the Andes on the night bus to Otavalo, Cat and her brothers were thrilled for me. But this growing old that is a change in the texture of life itself—who in their thirties would call this an adventure?

Most mornings Paul sits at the breakfast table in his red bathrobe, his reading glasses making his eyes look big as he clicks through his email and sips coffee from his big white mug. I sit across from him drinking jasmine tea from my red thermos and watching the blue jays fly in to fight for a place at the bird feeder. What could be more boring? And yet, well, I just have to laugh at the truth of it: in these most ordinary moments, the universe opens up. Universes, really. Because it's not the events that catch my attention, not those encapsulated, separate phenomena: "blue jays flying in," or "Paul drinking coffee." It's the texture of the living moments, each...what should I call it?

If I say "each instant" or "moment," you'll get the sense of a separate package of time and some event wrapped up like a birthday present or a stinking fish in newspaper or even old kitty litter, something you want or don't want or really don't want. But it's not like this anymore, not like a package you have an opinion about. Instead of instants or moments, here-and-nows are unfurling like fiddlehead ferns, tight little fists turning to feathery expanses of possibility.

Many days, the truth of getting old feels like these unfolding possibilities. There isn't one thing missing or any place I'd rather be than here. Can I tell this to Catherine? I couldn't have told it to myself at thirty, or even forty or fifty. I honestly never expected that simply being where I am and who I am would be enough, and that enough would feel like overflowing. It's not only that I didn't expect to feel this way in my sixties. I didn't imagine I could *ever* feel like this.

Private and Unsayable

This all seems like a secret I should be keeping. As I reflect on it, I see that sharing the reality of this time of life is not just about communicating the meaning of an experience to someone younger who has not yet had that experience. It's more that the *nature* of these experiences feels private. Not just untranslatable, but unsayable.

I long to be with others who know these secrets. My friend Jim told me to look at the poems that poets write toward the end of their lives. He quoted from W.S. Merwin's "Worn Words:"[2]

it is the late poems
that are made of words
that have come the whole way

"That's what I want," I told Jim, "to come the whole way through. It's a great thing we're living now, isn't it? Getting old I mean."

Jim flashed a conspiratorial smile, "It's a new frontier." Then he told me a dream he'd had the night before. Stick figures moved in a slow dance of controlled ecstasy, he said. As they danced, their heads and faces shifted through different forms, sometimes skulls and sometimes just empty shrouds and sometimes sheaves of wheat. "I was a little surprised that I wasn't scared," he said. "But actually, I was intrigued at the solemnity of it all, and I felt I was learning something fascinating."

Aging seems to be like this in its essence— leaving nothing out—not death, not emptiness, and not whatever harvest may come. Not pulling back half-grown at middle age but letting ourselves unfurl in an ecstatic dance we're just beginning to get the hang of.

Chapter 4

When Your Mind is Not Clouded

Ten thousand flowers in spring, autumn's harvest moon,
A cool breeze in summer, snow in winter.
When your mind is not clouded by unnecessary things,
Every season is the best season.
~Wu-Men Kui-k'ai [1]

On occasional summer mornings when I drive from my home in the sunny flatland of Novato to San Francisco, I almost always forget what will be waiting for me. Winding south around horses grazing on pale hills and straight on past the jumble of Sausalito's houseboats, I listen to NPR and enjoy the view. But once I reach the top of the Waldo Grade and gaze down to where the Golden Gate Bridge is supposed to be, I get a kind of shock. Only the tips of the bridge's orange-red pinnacles peek out. The rest is gone. The bridge and the city beyond—erased by a foggy, cold density. And I wonder, in some childlike place that takes life literally, why go on? Why not turn around right now and head back to the sunshine, the people, the stores, the place where all the good stuff is?

Do you ever feel this way about getting old? Like what is the point, after all? Can't we just turn the car around? Even if it hasn't been all sunshine and horses grazing on hillsides, so what? It's familiar, where we came from. We know who we are and what's expected of us there, the roads and the short cuts and where to get a quick cup of coffee. It's comforting to think of going where we've already been. Relaxing, in a way, not to have to cross that bridge where the road is hidden or gone.

I think we do this a lot—try to go where we've already been. Try, as Jung said, to live the evening's reality by what was true in the morning. And not only that. We also try to construct our future based on what we've seen of the past, in particular, on what we've seen of our elders' experience. It's so normal to forecast like this, building mental Lego constructions from whatever we've been impressed by — our grandfather's dementia, our aunt's sharp tongue, our grandmother's peaceful afternoons saying her rosary. We build our models unconsciously, and equally unconsciously, we try to take up residence in them. As if our impressions of aging and the constructions we make from them were real and true.

We believe in these mental models — in our ideas and beliefs and generalizations about aging — because we saw the aging with our own eyes and felt the loneliness of our grandfather and the grace of our grandmother with our own hearts. But actually, we don't know how our own aging will be because so much is different now. This seems so obvious, but it is not. We rarely notice that we have beliefs about aging, and we almost never question how those beliefs shape and limit our experience. It's as if we are enshrouded in the San Francisco fog; encumbered, as Zen Master Wu-men said eight centuries ago, by unnecessary things. And the life we could have, the best season of all, is hidden behind clouds.

* * *

It doesn't really matter how many books and articles we read, how many statistics and pie charts and red, green, and blue graph lines we stare at trying to make sense of what our aging means politically, socially, economically, or how many gerontologists, neuropsychologists, and other scientists explain to us what their research says about how our aging is going to be. To our soul, all that information is just numbers. What shapes our hopes and fears most intimately is our direct experience with our own elders.

How early did your impressions about aging start? If you're in your sixties or older, your ideas about aging were probably shaped by people born before 1900. If your grandparents lived to be as old as you are now, the way they cared for their bodies, their education, their opportunities to meet people of different faiths, cultures, and gender preferences; their perspectives on work, marriage, and retirement; the emotional intelligence they did or did not develop...well, you see where this is going. Why should you expect that your aging will be like theirs?

The answer is that we don't expect this—consciously. But unconsciously, we expect for ourselves what we witnessed as children. This impact continues into our teens because of the strong age segregation that exists in the West. It's even more true now than when we were children. How often do you find yourself hanging out with teenagers or twenty year olds? By our fifties, however, the hidden or recollected impressions from our childhood are joined by a powerful, second influence: the final years of our own parents' lives—if they survive long enough to grow old.

"I am constantly aware of an inner pessimism I have developed about aging," my friend Nick wrote from New York last winter. He apologized for being out of touch, explaining that he'd been accompanying his father through a long decline into dementia. "Having seen how difficult my father's final years became," he wrote, "I can't find anything positive or redemptive about growing old."

He said that he could see that we both had some time of richness ahead of us, but ended his email with a sentence that tore at my heart. "Personally," he wrote, "I am caught by a vision of the end years that is nothing to look forward to, and I haven't figured out a way to hold that future that is anything but somewhat grim."

I think it was the *somewhat* in Nick's final sentence that got me. The vulnerability of "somewhat," and the courage—willing to try for a different way of thinking if there is any sense to it, but dubious.

My mother's Alzheimer's disease was different. She became innocent, the shell of her pride melting away. When I entered her room at the nursing home, she'd light up with joy. When she bit into an orange, her eyes would fly open in wonder as the sweet juice burst onto her tongue. At times she was confused and anxious and it was very hard near the end, but for several years I was so happy to be with her. I'd longed for that closeness most of my life.

So as you can see, part of my experience with dementia is different from Nick's, and I am not so disheartened about what the future holds. Many of us have such definitive experiences with our parents. By the time we reach our sixties, however, virtually all of us have direct experiences of aging all the time. Our partners, friends, and colleagues are growing old, as we are. Some of us thrive. Others are in physical and/or mental decline. And a lot of us are some combination of all of the above, depending on the day.

You might think that now, finally, our childhood impressions would weaken their hold. But from what I can tell, they don't exactly fade. Rather, they are the scaffolding under our current experience. As I meet with elders, I often glimpse the early struts poking out. A management consultant from Colorado told me recently that she thinks about growing old a lot, constantly strategizing about it. When I asked why, she said that was what her father had done. It made her feel close to him, she said, tackling old age as he had.

Last month I was talking with a nurse from Australia. As she grows older, she said, she thinks about death all the time. Why all the time, I asked.

"Because," she said, "I'm afraid it's denial not to." I wondered where she got that idea. "In my family," she said, "we were in denial about so many of the big things in life. I don't want to be like that...so I guess I'm doing the reverse."

Do we ever get to have our own immediate experience of aging, unclouded by the past? Last summer, I thought I'd found it. It was near the end of a course I was teaching with Buddhist teacher Anna Douglas. Anna and I had divided the group of about a hundred elders into small groups according to their age decades. We asked them to reflect on a question about their experience of aging and report back. One person from each small group spoke except for the group in their eighties; every one of them stood up in turn to describe, with great exuberance, what she had discovered.

The last person, Melissa, explained: "All the rest of you are trying to find out what it's like to grow old," she said. "We already *are* old so we don't have to worry about it anymore!" And with a grand gesture of acknowledgement to her beaming cohort, she sat down, accompanied by laughter and enthusiastic applause.

I love remembering Melissa and the spirited response in the room that day. As I think about it now, however, I don't believe that reaching eighty, in itself, is an answer to being open to one's experience. Maybe it's *half* an answer. But it seems to me that clarity takes a lot more than simply getting old. It takes disengaging from the ties that bind us to the early experiences, and that takes some other things, like a willingness to recognize those ties, and name them, and feel how much they have meant and maybe still mean to us. It's tender work, this disentangling.

To understand the tenderness, and the tangles, think of the intimate foundations of our first concepts of aging. I remember the acrid smell of my grandfather's ever-present cigar and my delight when he lifted me high in the air in his office in downtown Philadelphia. And I remember how he framed (in gold!) my colored-in-the-lines drawing of Jack Frost *and* hung it on the wall right behind his desk. So when he got sick and weak and could no longer go to his office or pick me up when I came to visit, I formed a small certainty about what happens to old people. With such certainties and the emotional and sensory glue that secures them, we build our constructions about growing old. Hidden away by the elves of childhood, we take these constructs to be true. And so they remain safe and invisible, impervious to the rational information gathering of our adult minds.

It's not until we begin to look for these beliefs that we have a chance of uncovering them. Questions help a lot, like: *How do I know this idea about growing old is true?* And, *How would I feel if it wasn't?* And then it takes one more step to discover the feeder roots of those ideas, entwined and spidered around the memories of the ones we loved. Again, our curiosity can go into the hidden places, penetrating like solvent what seems to have been sealed shut. Here we can ask questions that go along with the secrets: *What's right about holding onto these ideas?* And, *What if I actually don't know how to grow old?*

Delving into the beliefs of the morning, as Jung might have put it, clears the way for the truth of the evening.

A Koan

As you can see, this obstacle is made not just from stories our culture feeds us but concepts constructed from our personal experience. The problem is not that we have concepts or even mental models of what our aging will be. The problem is that we take them to be true. We don't realize that what we have are generalizations from touching or vivid experiences with a few people who were important to us.

But we can definitely question, challenge, probe, and otherwise find out what we believe and where we got those ideas and whether, from what we can discover now, they are true.

One way to do this is with a koan. Koans are stories that pose a question to pester you. It gets under your skin, and you can't make it go away with your ordinary mind. You have to let yourself itch until something real shows up to scratch it. Not an answer exactly, but a knowing that springs from the source of the question itself. The story that follows is, I think, a koan about aging.

Harp Lessons

I heard this story when I was in my fifties from a good-looking blond bass player named Scott who was in a course I was taking. He wore a small gold ring in his left nostril and I thought he was incredibly cool. One day he invited me out for sushi after class. He said he'd heard I was interested in aging and wanted to talk to me.

"You look about thirty-five," I told him, puzzled. "How come you're interested in getting old?"

"I'm not, exactly," he said. "But I have something for you, a gift I think."

And then he told me a story he'd heard from his friend Akiro, a harpist, who had heard it from his teacher, who had heard it years earlier from her teacher, an old woman whose name Scott thought was Mildred but wasn't sure. The story was about a man whose name he did remember—Arthur Adolph Marx.

Here's how I remember the story:

Arthur was close to thirty when he was seized by a great longing to learn the harp. For some reason no one remembers any more, Arthur's mother sent him a harp, and he fell in love with the arc of it and the gold and the sounds the strings made when he plucked them. But the harp is an incredibly complex and difficult instrument to play. It has thousands of moving parts, all housed within a block of wood that is kept under pressure and will implode if not played regularly. There are strings and pedals and tuning knobs and sounding boards, and it's hard to tune.

Arthur tried anyway, for years. He couldn't find anyone to teach him, and he didn't know how to read music. He tuned the harp wrong and played it on the wrong shoulder. For all his efforts, he could not make the heavenly music he longed to hear.

So finally he went back to searching for a teacher.

"Forget it," one man told him. "You're far too old."

Another teacher went further, explaining, "In your thirties, it's impossible. Even at twenty—completely out of the question. You have to study the harp before you're twelve, before the structure of your hands sets and can no longer be shaped to the needs of the harp."

Others would insist on demonstrating to Arthur the utter hopelessness of his quest. Stretching their own elegant fingers into the wide claws needed to pluck the harp strings correctly, they would say, in effect, "You see? You see how it must be? Nothing personal, you understand, but don't even dream of learning to play this magical instrument at your age."

Arthur kept knocking on the doors of harp teachers, and they kept turning him away, one after the other, until one day he arrived at the home of a woman teacher. When he told her how weary he was and how long he had looked and how every teacher he met had refused him, she sat still, not saying a word. At last Arthur grew quiet too, and the teacher leaned forward and touched his arm.

"It's true what they say about the hands."

Arthur's bushy eyebrows descended, and his big child's eyes filled with tears.

"There's only one way open to you now," the teacher said.

Arthur's eyebrows flew up to his hairline. "There's a way? What is it? I'll do anything you tell me."

"It's very simple," she said. "You have to become a person of no age."

That very day, Arthur began his harp lessons. In time, his love and joy of playing changed him so profoundly that his name changed too. He became the great, ageless clown known as Harpo Marx.

Becoming A Person of No Age

"Harpo's teacher taught Akiro's teacher," Scotty told me as we finished our sushi, "and that's how I heard about becoming a person of no age. I thought you might need a story like this for the people who are growing old."

For a long time I thought the koan was this: How did Harpo do it? How did he become a person of no age? But I think I had it backward. The way it comes to me now, persistently, is this: What did Harpo stop doing? What did he let go of to become a person of no age?

Maybe he let go of carrying around all the concepts he had constructed about how old he was and what he couldn't do and how he had to be. I like to think that Harpo dropped those things—thunk!—like cheap white pottery shattering to the floor. Or if he couldn't drop them all right away, the possibility of becoming free was so tantalizing that he began to question every idea that came to his mind about how old he was and what that meant. Gradually, in my dreaming into this, Harpo's ideas about his age lost their power. Not that they disappeared. As long as you have a mind, you have thoughts about things. But maybe they became transparent and lost their power to cloud what he saw and shape who he was. They no longer defined him.

Whether or not Harpo's story is true in all of its tellings and retellings, it leaves us something to contemplate: We can be young, and we can be old, and we can sometimes be a person of no age, all within a day, all within an hour. The point is not to try to become a person of no age. That's just one more concept. The point is to be free to live the fullness of our lives, whatever our age. Bill Marx, Harpo's son, describes his father as someone who took in the world with wonder, for whom everything was new.[2] As Zen Master Wu-Men put it—ten thousand flowers in spring, the moon in autumn.

Chapter 5

Escaping Mother Culture's Web

But the human mind no the human mind has
nothing to do with age. As I say so, tears come into my eyes.
Gertrude Stein, *Geographical History of America*[1]

While it is wonderful to have a mind that is free from concepts, it's not enough. In our over-informed and complicated era, we get caught again and again in the great tangled web of those concepts, and especially the ones about aging. To break free, we need to look very carefully at who is weaving this web. Who is managing to hijack our most personal experiences, snatching our intimate moments and weaving them into her own meanings?

The master weaver is Mother Culture. Truly skillful and elusive, she is almost invisible because she is the fabric that holds our mainstream lives together—the blog lore and news stories and gossip columns and films and marketing of just about everything. Her countless nuances murmur endlessly, interpreting our experience, including, of course, our experience of aging. If we somehow fall or crawl out of her web, she extends her hand casually and we take it, barely noticing how willingly we slip back into the special place set aside for our stage of life.

And one more thing: Mother Culture is always right. At least she thinks she is, and usually we believe her. She's sure that she's the only one with common sense and most of the time, most of us agree. For thousands of years, the beliefs that represent our conventional side claim that, more than any other thing, they make us *safe*. If we stay close to Mother Culture, our ancestors believed, she'll keep us from starving when there are famines, and she'll keep us healthy when there are plagues. Don't make waves, we learned. Don't challenge the status quo. Color inside the lines, and everything will work out for the best.

In Daniel Quinn's *Ishmael*, the teacher (who happens to be a large silver-backed gorilla) explains to his student that it's possible to escape Mother Culture's web. You have to pay close attention, he says, and then you can hear her constant story-telling humming in your ears. Once you do, "you'll never stop being conscious of it. Wherever you go for the rest of your life, you'll be tempted to say to the people around you, 'How can you listen to this stuff and not recognize it for what it is?'" When the student protests that it's a little hard to believe there *is* such a story, the gorilla "close[s] his eyes gently in an indulgent smile. 'Belief is not required. Once you know this story, you'll hear it everywhere.'"[2]

And so we can. Once we know the story, we can hear it humming everywhere. And more importantly, we can choose to step out of it.

Almost always, this starts with confusion or embarrassment. You feel that you're not fitting in the way you're supposed to, and it's probably your fault. Let's say that you don't push yourself back where you used to be. By luck or courage, you stay right there, paying attention to what you feel and see. That's when something different can happen. You start to know what you don't want to know about yourself—your judgments and projections about old people, for example. You feel things—fear or passion or hatred or tenderness. And for maybe the first time ever, you spot the invisible stage markings that have kept you and everybody you know in their places in our cultural drama: the lovely ingénue, the wizened crone, the crotchety old man, the one who is too young, the one who is too old.

Sunnybrook

When I was thirty-eight, a youngish psychologist in the middle of my so-called career, I signed on for what turned out to be an immersion course in my cultural prejudices about old people. It was my first big step out of a story that I hadn't noticed I was inhabiting. I wasn't trying to step out of that story. All I knew was that something seemed to be wrong with my life, and I needed to do something about it.

I'd sit in my nice corner office at the biggest psychiatric research institute in Canada and hold my new book on my lap. It was called *Crazy Talk*. Based on ten years of my research on schizophrenic thought disorder, it was receiving good reviews in the academic journals and had gotten me a big promotion. But when I thought about those ten years of research and what I had written, I doubted that anyone was going to benefit from it. And one more thing was bothering me—the distance that always seemed to exist between doctors (us) and patients (them), between researchers (us) and subjects (them). I had started to feel my own acute symptoms of this separation: loneliness.

So I sat around and wondered what I could do, or join, to not feel so divided from the people I spent most of my days talking to. Then I got a call from an old friend inviting me to be part of a team in psycho-geriatrics. What's that, I asked. Old people, he said. You'll help us design research to learn about old people.

I jumped at the chance, sure that studying aging was just what I needed. We won't be able to imagine that our subjects aren't like us, I thought. We are going to get old, just like they are. They are us in a few decades. So I left my cushy job at the University of Toronto for a little chronic care hospital in the suburbs called Sunnybrook. Going to help people, I hoped, and get beyond separations.[3]

It wasn't so easy. Where I'd been head of my department and had a lot of support at my old job, I was rather lost once I got to the hospital. My team was busy caring for patients and needed little of my time. I hung around and tried not to get in the way. Eventually I started a few therapy groups and visited whatever patients felt like talking to me.

A Woman Called Red

Red was a patient on the pulmonary ward, an ex-smoker who had lost an arm to gangrene from her smoking. She couldn't go anywhere without her oxygen tank. The tank was on wheels so she could roll it through the hospital corridors when she went for a walk.

Red's nickname seemed incongruous to me because everything about her was bleached out. She had whitish hair, skin like a crumbled, white paper bag and pale legs so skinny it was painful to watch her move. She's hardly here at all, I thought, and for some reason I couldn't account for, I found her intensely irritating.

"Red never talks," I complained to one of the nurses. "Is she mentally competent?"

"Don't underestimate Red," the nurse replied tartly.

I sighed noisily. One more elusive ghost. I preferred the old men who brightened up when I came into their rooms and always had time to talk.

Writing this now, I see something I couldn't then. I wasn't just an irritable young psychologist. I was a woman trying to keep it together with a very tired husband in law school who was working part time on the side, and two gorgeous, teenaged stepdaughters bursting with energy. I was working full time and cooking for our family and cleaning the house when I got around to it. I may have been in my thirties but I felt, I moaned to my friends, decrepit—as in ramshackle, dilapidated, ruined from old age and neglect.

Red terrified me. I did not want to look across the decades to see someone who looked as wrecked as I already felt. And I definitely did not want to see what, in my worst moments, I imagined my future held: the ghostly, washed-out and washed-up fate of women who grow old.

But then I spied Red doing something alarming, something that was to shake up my tight little opinions. Late in the afternoon when the day shift was over, I was working with my office door open when I spotted Red pushing her oxygen tank quickly along the corridor in a move that reminded me of the scuttling of a hermit crab. I peeked out just in time to see her disappear through the French doors to the outside balcony. I hurried after her and stopped just inside the doors, in the shadows.

Silhouetted against the setting sun, Red coolly yanked the oxygen tube out of her nostrils, turned off the tank and shoved the whole apparatus away from her. It glided across the balcony and bumped into a stone urn. And then, to my horror, Red pulled a package of cigarettes and a book of matches from her pocket. Resting back against the balcony as if she were leaning against a railing of the Ile de France, she tapped a cigarette out of the pack, slipped it between her lips, and with a single-handed flick of a match, lit it. Rita Hayworth in all her glory could not have matched Red as she tossed back her head and took a long, sensuous inhale.

I was appalled. And thrilled. Sneaking looks through the glass doors, I felt my heart thumping at the pure outrageousness of what she was doing. She's killing herself, I thought. I've got to stop her.

She doesn't have many years left, another voice retorted. Leave her alone. My heart was with the second voice. I turned and walked back down the hall, leaving Red exhaling smoke rings into the sunset.

It wasn't too long after that, about a month I think, that my certainties about Red got shaken again. Her son and daughter-in-law flew in from Montreal, carrying a large photo album with them. Not for Red, they told us, but for you, the nurses and doctors and the other staff. "To show you who she was and still is," her son said. "So you don't just think she's a washed-out old lady who's never had a life before becoming a patient at Sunnybrook Hospital."

I crowded in with a few of the nurses to look at the album. How glamorous she had been, shapely legs in high heels with open toes, a flame of hair flung back, laughing, gesturing with an ever-present cigarette floating in her hand.

When she saw us all bent over the album, Red made her way over, pushing the oxygen tank ahead of her. "Pretty hot, wasn't I?" she said, claiming her due.

"You were something else!" the nurses told her. She leaned over with us as we peered at photograph after photograph of her in dresses of emerald green and electric blue with heels and purses to match. But never a hat. Only that fiery crown curling down to her shoulders, matching her lipstick. Set off by a few good-looking men.

Red was happy for the attention that day and after that, something shifted between us. She still didn't talk to me much, but we seemed to have an understanding. I didn't bother her and she nodded agreeably from time to time.

Something else shifted too—the blithe projection of my age fears onto Red. Before I saw the photo album and certainly before I spotted Red on the balcony in her Ile de France solitude, I had written her off. Not consciously. It was worse than that. I had erased her from the realm of people to talk to, to hear stories from, even to sit and watch soap operas with. The separations I had been so eager to leave behind—I was carrying with me. I was embarrassed and unhappy, seeing all of this, but I figured I was learning a lot about myself and the territory of old age.

That was before I discovered how much I had to learn from the old men. As I mentioned, I liked being with the men from the very beginning. But after a few months, I moved from the pulmonary ward to one where there were quite a number of men. When I walked into their coffee room, they smiled at me like the sun itself was coming to warm them. I brightened, met by their teasing and laughter and evident welcome. It seemed to have something to do with fire and light—the lightness that ignited when my (relatively) young female self came into the presence of those old men. Suddenly I needed new skirts. And tops. And shoes. Out went my black skirts, camel-hair suit, and grey almost everything for an armload of new clothes. All of them tighter. Most of them red. I wore a lot of red that year.

Just sitting and talking with the men opened a life force in me that I hadn't felt since adolescence. Or maybe ever. And it wasn't just aliveness that I was feeling. Though I never put this into words, even to myself. I can tell you that I felt like I was one of the sexier women on earth. When I walked (okay, flounced) onto those geriatric wards, the men looked at me like they wanted to make love to me. That was exactly what I wanted too. I wanted to give it away, to give them this pulsing youth that had marvelously, mysteriously sprung alive in me. (This is called acting out if you do it. If you just think it...let's see: normal, I'd say, for a late-thirties self-described decrepit woman just starting to discover her inner love goddess.)

I have no trouble recalling this now, when I am as old as the men were then. I must have been half-crazed that year, untethered from the harness that had kept me in my good sane normal roles. Miraculously I suppose, I never did act it out. But I remember my compelling conviction that if I could make love with those men, I would somehow be able to make them young again. Save them from dying. I wonder if they dreamed that too. Years later when I read about sacred prostitutes serving the Great Goddess in the temples of India and the ancient Near East, I felt a kinship.

My friends were amazed at how I was thriving on the chronic wards of a geriatric hospital. I just smiled. I couldn't imagine what I would say. It's only now that I see how young I was. Not so much in years but in maturity of heart. My own fears of being old and unlovable had shut me down to Red and to anyone else who wasn't outgoing and interested in me. And yet, those old men with their response to a young woman brought life to me in a way I'd given up on. It was what the anthropologist Mary Catherine Bateson called "a fruitful reciprocity," happening beyond Mother Culture's meanings, and certainly beyond the boundaries of my own young life.

A Zone of Freedom

As I look back on that time, I see that I was beginning to step into a zone of freedom, to venture outside Mother Culture's walls of age and develop a taste for meeting others there. One of my first experiments was with my mother-in-law, Gwen. I had an early meeting scheduled in Oakville, a town about an hour from my home and where Gwen lived. On a whim, I left extra early so I could stop by to visit with her. This was a very odd whim because Gwen and I had a rather formal relationship with each other. We'd never been alone in the several years I'd been her son's second wife. I don't think we'd even had a personal conversation, just the two of us. Our meetings were always in the living room in the midst of a family party or when I helped to serve Christmas dinner on her silver platters. And certainly I'd never seen Gwen without perfectly coiffed hair, "put together," as she would have said, in one of her elegant suits, with stockings, high heels, and perfectly manicured nails.

This is what stepping out of Mother Culture's net can do: I stopped at a phone booth and called. It was around 8 a.m. Gwen answered, a little taken aback with my enthusiasm for an early morning visit, but ever gracious, she said, "Of course dear. Come right over."

When I rang, she opened the door in her bathrobe and slippers. I'd never seen her without makeup. "I hope it's okay," I said. "I just thought we might be able to have a cup of tea together before my meeting."

"Oh yes," she said. "Come in, come in."

What an odd and precious time that was. We sat next to each other on her living room sofa, drinking tea from her bone china cups and nibbling on toast with raspberry preserves set on the coffee table. We were blessedly unimpeded, as I recall it now, by the stiff roles we'd always worn with each other. We hadn't exactly dropped those roles. They simply evaporated as if they'd never existed. We spoke with ease, touching on deep matters and light ones, laughing at times. I remember having a sense once or twice of reaching out for an invisible wall that used to be there, and finding nothing. Just space.

I was sorry to leave that day, to let go of the pleasure of strolling with this fascinating woman in a field where the walls that had divided us were gone. When that strong, opinionated, dear woman I'd come to love very much was dying a few years later, I sat by her hospital bed for many hours. She was in a coma, but it seemed to me that we had no trouble meeting in that field we had found together, early in the morning, when the walls fell down.

Chapter 6

Secrets & Subtleties

Walker, there is no road.
Only wind trails in the sea.
~Antonio Machado[1]

As we look into the obstacles to our maturing, it's easy to see why they block our way. After all: lies, death, early imprints we can't remember, and late ones we'd like to forget—who wouldn't hurry past as quickly as possible and fill her days with more cheerful pursuits?

And yet...there is something. Many things really. Growing older, we have some experiences that intrigue us and others we find poignant or funny or deeply perplexing. At times, we want to share these with a friend, or even a stranger. Why is that? What do we think it will give us—telling another person and hearing how it is for them, too?

The Ones We Share Easily

It's pretty obvious why we like to talk to each other about the stories our culture spins. They really are fun to expose—their shiny or hangdog faces sticking out for everyone to see. When we get mad and laugh about them together, they're less likely to sneak up and make themselves at home in our bathroom mirror. And telling each other how we get caught turns out to be a splendid ice-breaker.

I drove over to a film studio north of San Francisco one October day in 2009, not in the best of moods. I'd agreed to be interviewed by a friend of a friend about my views on women. I was feeling very introverted that day and rather blank, wondering why on earth I said I'd do this. For protection, I'd brought my mother's red cashmere shawl to wrap around me. My interviewer came in a bit late, apologizing and looking a bit harried. As she settled across from me, she pulled a beautiful blue-green shawl around her shoulders. Is she nervous too, I wondered.

She introduced herself—Celedra, from Portland. As we were waiting for the mike and camera checks, she told me how last week she'd been lying across her bed, reading to her four-year-old grandson, Jacob, when she noticed him peering worriedly at her arm. "So I stop reading and join him in looking at my arm," she said. "'Lala,' he tells me gravely, 'you know, there is a cream I saw on TV and if you buy it and put it on your arm every night, your arm will look just like mine in nine weeks, instead of all wrinkly.'"

We'd just met and already we were laughing together and feeling like friends. She went on to tell me that a few days later, she was driving Jacob's sister Celia to ballet lessons when she saw Celia gazing at her with the same kind of worried look. "She wanted to know if when she gets old her cheeks are going look like they do now, like her own skin, she said, or will they look like mine."

My new friend sighed. "I thought grandchildren were supposed to love you so totally that they don't notice stuff like wrinkles. I don't know where I got that idea!"

The Ones We Tend to Hide

While stories are easy to share, the concepts that underlie them are not. For one thing, many concepts about aging are invisible to us, even though they influence about a zillion behaviors. For another, when they do surface, they tend to be...well, embarrassing or painful, or both. We all have these fears lurking nearby and probably flitting through our mind several times a day: fear of being a burden as we get old; suspicion that we're becoming tedious; worries about how we'll manage if our spouse is diagnosed with Alzheimers. And, as you probably know too well, even if you want to share these thoughts, your friends don't necessarily want to hear them.

In one of my inquiry groups for elders, I became curious about a big Dutchman with a white bush of a beard who arrived early to each meeting. At the end of the first night, he announced that his name was Ron, he lived in a small town up north, and would appreciate a ride to the downtown bus station. When he continued to ask for a ride to the bus at the end of every meeting, I realized how long he must have to travel to get to us. Finally, I thought to ask him to tell us why he was going to so much trouble.

I remember that he sighed and looked down at his hands for a while. He told us that he had started several men's groups for elders in his town. "It always looked promising in the beginning," he said. "The men seemed glad for a chance to talk and exchange stories. But once we got to the hard stuff—what scared us about getting old, how we felt about dying alone, and what I've decided are the two most terrible words in the English language: nursing homes—they stopped coming. Just fell like leaves in winter and didn't even call to say why. But I knew. It's bloody hard to talk about these things, as much as we need to."

The room was silent when he finished. Sober. I sensed a respect for what he had been through, again and again trying to create a community, a circle, some place to share the truth of what it is like growing old. I felt grateful to him. We'd been exploring fears like these but hadn't acknowledged how much courage it took, and how much we needed the safe environment we created to hold our fears.

Here's the most important part, I think. For many of us, if there is no one who can listen with generosity and respect to what Ron calls the hard stuff, we don't listen to ourselves. We are not able to look at our fears and welcome our feelings if we believe we are alone. I know this has been true for me and for many women I've met. I think it is true for men, too, even if they find the vulnerability more daunting. Because as lonely as it is to have no one to confide in, it's far lonelier to be separated from ourselves.

The Ones We Don't Have Words For

Some of our experiences of aging are easy to share, and some are hard but others are not exactly easy or hard. We rarely talk about them at all because there seem to be no words that fit. These experiences are not so much secret as they are subtle, soul-level truths from what Jung calls the evening of our life. From the perspective of the truth of the morning, they are paradoxical and confusing. We tend not to share these with anyone, not even our closest friends. And that is a great loss because these realities, richer and more mysterious than anything we expected, are the growing edge of our ripening.

Last August I had a visit from Miriam, one of my former students who had moved to the East Coast. She said that she wanted to tell me about what she called "some interesting changes" in her life. The changes turned out to be directly at this growing edge.

"I'm in an unfamiliar landscape," Miriam began, settling herself in the big rocking chair in my consulting room. "Can you imagine waking up with a sense of wonder every day? Can you imagine," she leaned forward, "me, at seventy-three, feeling this way?"

I felt a stinging sensation of tears I was holding back. No, I couldn't imagine it, but I wanted to. I wanted to hear how Miriam had found her way to wonder after decades of doubting herself and her vocation as a rabbi, after a hard divorce and a recent year of moving through bankruptcy.

I waited, wanting her to be able to lay out her story like a dress pattern on the floor, fastening it carefully to the fabric of her life so far, cutting through the layers with good scissors. It takes time to let the shape of a story emerge distinctly—time to tell it and time to hear it.

Eventually she was ready. Sometime during the bankruptcy year, she said, she decided to stop hiding and stop lying.

"I never thought you lied," I told her mildly.

"I lied to myself," she replied, quietly. Miriam was never emotional, but something was different. She had a kindness and objectivity toward herself that I never saw before.

"There was the shame of the bankruptcy and the pain of it and blaming myself and anyone else I could think of. It was like I had let some feral cats slip inside my skin, and finally I just got sick of the clawing and scratching and threw them out." She gave the rocking chair a push or two and rested back into it. I sipped my tea and looked out at the redwoods to check on how they were doing in the heavy heat. Tattered edges of brown showed through the branches, making the trees look worn and tired.

Miriam interrupted my mental gardening. "You know what happens when you stop all that frantic doing?" she said. "You feel hopeless. Like you've given up and now there's nothing left to believe in. Then you stop, and the grief comes. I just let it in, the ache and the pain and finally the tears." She paused for a while. "The tears felt good, like rain after a long drought."

I nodded, wondering if she hit the emptiness that can come after all the running stops.

"Then there wasn't anything," she said. "I'd feel disintegrated or some days like a hollowed-out Halloween pumpkin with the shell all pulpy and caving in. But I'd given up fighting, you know. I just went through my days doing what I needed to do and feeling...empty."

I know, I thought, keeping my mouth shut so I didn't get in her way. I know how it is to feel scooped out, vacant, not standing for or against anything. I used to get so frantic when I felt that emptiness coming near.

"And then it started to change," she said. "I didn't do

anything but I felt relaxed, like something was opening inside me that I could trust." She looked at me steadily. "I feel that way now."

I waited.

"There's more," she said. "Like I told you, I'm living in a new landscape. I feel confident in a way I never have before. But it's not like I have a map."

She smiled a little awkwardly, at the paradox I suppose, feeling confident when you don't know where you're going. I asked her about the confidence.

"It's like I'm sure-footed no matter how rocky the path, how fogged in or overgrown or whatever. I have a trust I never had before that once I take a step, it will be okay. And if I need to change what I'm doing, I will."

"Wind trails," I murmured.

"What?"

"A poem by Machado. 'There is no road,' he says, 'You make the road by walking.' And he says, what you thought were roads are 'only wind trails in the sea.'"

She considered this. "Yeah, sort of. But he makes it sound as if it's too bad but that's how reality is —nothing to guide you. You just have to step along blindly, like in those dreams I used to have of being lost. That's what is different now."

I looked at her. Her grey eyes were shining and wide open. How do you describe an openness that looks like 10,000 miles with no clouds? Like clear sailing without an end? Or rather, like knowing that whatever the sailing—torrential rains or forty-foot-high crests and troughs or becalmed, you're here for it. Not holding back. Not doubting yourself, fretting about whether you should be in some other place doing some other thing.

We may be walking on wind trails, I wanted to tell her, but you're the opposite of lost. I didn't bother. She already knew.

The Space at The Center

This season of our lives is new. Why is it so hard to remember this, I ask myself. Why are we so surprised to find ourselves in the midst of paradox, the conventional reality no longer a good fit for the truth we're living? I feel impatient with myself, with the words and the images I've been using about explorers stepping into a new country.

I want to throw all those metaphors out (a bit rash! I'd be mute, but you get the idea.) Here's the problem: to say that we're explorers entering new territory is fair enough until we get to the soul level of maturing. Then it doesn't make sense to talk as if we have been ambling along through our lives and now we're just going to walk on a bit further, across the Marin County line into Sonoma, say, and create a new map.

It's not like that at all. Not really. Not if we recognize what it means to be pinned against our death, rooted to it. Something fundamental is shifting now, whether our inner seismograph detects the movement or not. What is shifting is not simply the landscape. It is *us*.

I like the way Miriam put it: at some point, who you suppose you are and how you suppose you have to be empties out like a Halloween pumpkin. Or you could think about bananas. You know how the bananas you buy at the grocery store these days have specially treated pieces of plastic on the ends to prevent ripening? Before you can actually eat a banana, the day before at least, you have to peel off the plastic. And—it seems obvious—so do we. Need to peel off, I mean, whatever has been keeping us unripe.

That peeling away almost always leaves us feeling empty. But as the poet Chana Bloch says:

There's no way to change
without touching
the space at the center of everything.[2]

We forget that we're already naked.

What makes it so hard to remember that this season of our lives in this era of our human evolution is new? It's this: the way we clutch onto our ideas about growing old as if they were our only truth instead of plastic coverings that keep us from ripening. Once we get interested in what's developing, we're less inclined to fight the ways we're changing and it's an immense relief.

But then do we become unrecognizable to ourselves? Perhaps we do in a way. Miriam is no longer the woman who doubted herself and everything else. If her forty-year-old self could have time-traveled ahead thirty years, she might walk right past the luminous, confident old woman she is today, not even recognizing the one she has become.

Open and Closed

D.H. Lawrence wrote of "new, strange flowers such as my life has not brought forth before" even as he was ill and weary near the end of his life. So much openness is needed to welcome what we are becoming—"new blossoms of me" Lawrence called it—while the rest of aging is happening too.[3]

It's a great stretch to include it all; to want to know ourselves completely, not choosing one way of being over another. As we've seen, there are many obstacles to this embrace. To end this section, I want to tell you about one of the most common—and to my mind pernicious—holes we fall into. I encounter this one constantly, in my friends and colleagues, my family and of course in myself. It showed up again last month, when my friend Marcia and I took a trip to Lake Tahoe.

Marcia lives in Alaska, not far from Anchorage. I've grown to love the deep well of silence she carries within her, and I was happy that we would have time to visit together and write and hike a bit. We had just had birthdays—my sixty-ninth and Marcia's sixtieth—so we talked, as women do, about this time in our lives. She told me that she and her husband used to travel every winter to beautiful places around the world—Belize, Australia, Mexico, the Philippines, Hawaii. But in the last year or so, she said, she has felt so happy staying at home.

We were strolling alongside a pretty little stream, and Marcia stopped to admire it. Then she said, with some concern in her voice, "Still, I find myself wondering if something is wrong with me, not wanting to travel like we used to. Maybe I'm just getting old."

"Maybe I'm just getting old."

When I hear those words, I am no longer a normal person. I become a raving maenad ready to tear the person who uttered them to pieces with my bare hands (or maybe my teeth. Yes, my teeth!).

NOTHING HAPPENS "JUST" BECAUSE WE'RE GETTING OLD. I want to scream that.

WHEN WE WANT SOMETHING NEW, WHY DO WE ASSUME SOMETHING IS WRONG WITH US? I want to yell that too.

DON'T ASSUME YOU KNOW WHAT IS HAPPENING!

DON'T ASSUME IT'S BAD!

FIND OUT!

You get the idea. I didn't actually shout at my dear friend right there on the public path in downtown Truckee with all the kids running around and couples walking their dogs. I calmed down and waited till we'd had dinner and a glass of Merlot. Marcia laughed when I told her, but she listened too. "How are we going to let the mystery of our lives open up if we keep slamming the door on it with that horrid maybe-I'm-just-getting-old mantra?" I asked her. (It wasn't really a question but at least I didn't yell.)

Afterward, as we walked into the cold with the stars sharp in the mountain sky, we talked for a long time about how easy it is to stuff the unknown into a box labeled "getting old" and lock it away. As if we already know everything we ever needed or wanted to know about our lives. As if we could plot the wind trails, and map the space at the center of everything.

Chapter 7

Pentimento

One balmy morning in late July, I'm sitting curled on the chintz sofa in our living room, content as a cat in the sun. I've been gazing through our picture window, admiring my potted roses in full bloom on the porch. A light breeze shivers the sheets of poplars in the distance and drifts through our open windows. Then—amazing—a slap of wet, cold ocean air stings my face and a whiff of brine wrinkles my nose as if I were catapulted back to the Atlantic City beaches of my childhood. How is this possible—a winter wind flinging its salty self across half a century of time and a continent of space into my California living-room?

I ponder this for some days. I don't tell anyone, not even Paul, because what would I say? But I find myself wondering, like my friend Marcia did: Is this about getting old? But because I had such a fit when Marcia asked the question, I don't dare drop it. Taking my own advice for a change, I'm willing to let this odd experience tickle my curiosity. Is it really possible that the boundaries separating distance and time soften, or open, as we grow old? What's happening here?

My curiosity becomes like fingers delicately tickling deep into my consciousness. And what comes to mind, in the mysterious way that memory delivers its packages, is my friend Joan and what she called pentimento.

I was living in Canada then, in my early thirties. Joan, who seemed very old indeed, was in her late fifties. She was short, stout, and a very strong walker. She liked to remind her friends that she'd been a WAC sergeant in World War II and bragged about being able to read topo maps. We enjoyed hiking together and had just finished a longish trek through the hills of southern

Ontario. It must have been June because school was out and wildflowers were everywhere. We were resting, I remember, lying back on a grassy hillside and gazing out at a field of willowy flowers with tiny white blossoms at their center.

"Queen Anne's Lace," Joan told me.

I was admiring them in the enthusiastic way I had for just about everything in those days, remarking on the delicacy of the little petals and how gracefully the flowers swayed on their thin stems. "Where you see the flowers," Joan said, "I see a pentimento."

She had a rough, almost mannish voice. Sometimes it was hard to tell if she was angry or just feeling some emotion she didn't care to express. I thought I heard something of the latter when she said that interesting word.

"It's a painter's term," Joan explained. "Canvas is so expensive that artists sometimes paint over their old pieces to have fresh surfaces. For a while, this works just fine. The new painting completely obscures the old one. But in time the top layers grow transparent with age and the earlier images bleed through. That's pentimento."

"Pentimento," I repeated, feeling the pleasant staccato on my tongue.

She told me that the word comes from the Italian meaning repentance, because the painter had given his composition some thought and then wanted something else. "But still, after some time, the original is there too," she said. "So you never lose it, even though it looks for a long time like it has gone."

We sat together not saying anything, watching the swaying field of white. "Where you see this hillside," Joan said finally, "I see this one...and others." Her voice wavered. "I see Lucy, when she was five, the year before she died, skipping and laughing and almost hidden as she ran through the Queen Anne's Lace, making it shake and bend and then laughing some more."

She watched the breeze ruffle the flowers. "That memory

layers over the same fields after she died, when I stomped through the Queen Anne's Lace, crushing it under my boots like weeds. Reamed out and devastated. And now, sitting here with you," she looked up at me, her eyes wet, "I'm enjoying the freshness of the morning, and your good company, and the beauty of that selfsame flower."

She sighed. "That's how it is now. Behind one reality lie deeper, more private ones. None of it is lost. It's all here right now. Textured." She paused. "And poignant."

I nodded, impressed. That's what happens when you get old, I thought. I worried a little that all that bleeding through might get in the way of just sitting on a hillside on a summer morning. Still, I hoped I'd experience such rich and complicated layerings when I grew old.

Surprises and Secrets

Over the years, running on a country road or hiking through the hills, I'd sometimes encounter the white faces of Queen Anne's Lace bobbing in the wind or standing erect in drainage ditches in the morning sun. "Pentimento," I'd whisper, and imagine memories transparent as veneer, one shining sheet over another.

But now, as I near seventy, I see that I had it wrong. Or if not wrong, at least a little bit off as I find with so many things about actually growing old, as opposed to my ideas of what it would be like. What it's actually like, the pentimento Joan described so long ago, is more...well, shimmering, more alive and instantaneous than I had imagined. The way I know pentimento today is not a brittle crackling like veneer breaking up; or musty and stiff the way old wallpaper gets; and it's not really texturing either, as if we were tapestries being woven by our life's events. Those are just metaphors I made up to try to understand what I hadn't lived.

Whatever I experienced last July on my sofa isn't exactly pentimento, I decide. It's not layerings but some opening in the time-space continuum of consciousness, instantaneous and distinctly itself. That briny smell was unmistakable, and so was the cold, wet smack of wind on my face. What are these moments, I wonder. My brain deteriorating?

I feel how delicate this inquiry is. If I take what I experience now, the newness of it, as a problem to worry about or take to my doctor... My mind plays with this for a bit. I feel dull, tired, somewhat gloomy. Oh—aha! It's my old friend, "Old age is boring." Now I'm almost laughing, delighted to spot what is going on. Okay then, I'm getting clear. This habit of seeing anything new in my experience as trouble is spoiling the reality I'm living. It is shutting me down.

So turn around, I tell myself. Let's just be here, interested. Open.

That's better. My curiosity springs back, alert and looking around. I still don't know what these openings are or what they might allow as I spend time contemplating them. I don't know how what I am—my usual identity of an almost seventy-year-old woman sitting in her living room, roses on the front porch, husband in the kitchen making lunch—might open too. I don't know whether the path I think I'm walking on will turn out to be narrow or wide or no path at all.

Untranslatable Meanings

There are so many depths to be plumbed as we age. And these depths—ours to fathom, if we will—seem to be hidden from our younger selves. What I knew in my twenties and thirties and forties lacked whole dimensions of the reality that is unfolding now.

Maybe we need a code word that could point to the untranslatable experiences and mysteries we face as we age. Pentimento, for example might be one of those words. We could use it to signal each other when something was happening that might just be too hard to explain to the uninitiated. Like the way a whiff of a gardenia bush in North Carolina can ambush you back fifty years to Atlantic City, New Jersey. Suddenly, you're in your prom gown with the avocado-green silk sash and the wide-net skirts, pulling open a white box the florist has just delivered, and your mother is standing behind you and you can hardly breathe for the heavy, clingy, sweet scent and the excitement of it all.

How do we talk about a shift of sensations like this, so immediate, so permeating, that reality itself is changed? Could we instead just murmur our code word — *Pentimento!* — and instantly any elders around would understand and nod sagely or twinkle or whatever it is we are supposed to do? Or, since there are so many secrets like this, we could just relax and give up trying to communicate something before its time has come. If not exactly secrets, then perhaps we could call them subtleties with untranslatable meanings. Like the way that any random perfume or touch or music can be a time-machine, flinging open the time-space vector. And the fact that, what you used to think of as Events with their own separate boxes and more or less reliable walls, become fluid, their walls permeable, their contents flowing into one another. And here's one more fact or, if you will, secret: You may start to love this unpredictability. Not knowing when a wall will dissolve, you might abandon your loyalty to the conventional categories of childhood and middle age and old. You might, at times, become a person of no age.

It's not that we have never before had glimpses of this fluidity of events and permeability in our sense of self and the systems we live in. But once we pass fifty or sixty or somewhere along in there, it gets more obvious. The times in my life I used to think needed to be packaged up and labeled or they would get away from me are doing just that — soaking through the boxes I put them in. The boxes turn out to be made of cardboard anyway, wet cardboard actually, so soft that I can't take them seriously anymore.

Moreover, "memories" are not what I used to think they

were—scenes and stories of things that happened in the past. My experiences, memories included, are more like watercolors laid transparently over each other. Not in a muddy way, though. Somehow the layers keep their distinctness, the way that herbs enhance a savory dish. So are memories water colors or herbs? I wave my hand dismissively. Memories are what they are, and I'm just trying to convey some of the secret and subtle meanings truer than words.

PART III

CULTIVATION

cultivate, vt (L. from colere, to cultivate, worship)

The origin of *cultivate* has a surprising meaning: *worship*. Our ancestors regarded cultivation as sacred work. Breaking up crusty soil, pulling weeds, feeding and watering and nurturing so the promise waiting in the seeds could be fulfilled—all this was seen as holy. And so, perhaps surprising too, I propose that the practice of asking and following our soul-deep questions is a holy, worthwhile, precious occupation. Holy because it prepares the ground for what we can be. Worthwhile because it supports our ripening. And precious because, when we engage our questions, we can open to what is true and real in a human life. What could be more valuable than that?

As we saw in the last few chapters, recognizing the obstacles that block our way is a necessary first step to ripening. Once we unearth the roots, obstacles tend to lose their power. Instead of being bored by aging, we get interested. Instead of assuming we know all about growing old, we become curious. Even our fear of death can transform from an obstacle to a catalyst to ripening, as I discuss in Chapter 10. And our personal and cultural stories about aging don't disappear, but they no longer have to blindside us.

So now we can turn toward the next step: *cultivation*. I like the way this word sneaks in the possibility of our becoming good gardeners. Still, I'm not so sure about the connotations of hacking up surface soil and killing weeds and so on. Just thinking about all that effort makes me tired. Even *development*, defined as *to cause to grow,* seems awfully strenuous. My favorite name for what this next step entails comes from the Old French verb *develloper,* meaning to *unfold and unwrap.* I imagine us as gardeners providing good soil and a shady location for our ferns so they can send down good roots, and unfurl eventually into feathery green magnificence. The gardener doesn't cause the unfurling and neither do we. Unfurling is our nature. We're just allies in the process, cultivating what is already underway.

In this section, we'll explore ways to cultivate what is ripening in us. Being present to our actual experience—that's one way. Wanting to know more about that experience—that's another, and it can enhance the first. A third way and key to all the others is learning to follow our questions. All of these have been important to me and to the elders I've worked with over the years. But at times these ways are closed to us. We're just too stuck in our certainties, too oblivious or naïve, too pig-headed to be able to walk through the easy gates. That's what happened to me. My process of cultivation, if you can call it that, began with a gate that led straight to the underworld.

Chapter 8

Disturbing the Furies

In 1992, the year I turned fifty, I was invited to Toronto to be a keynote speaker at a conference for women. The conference organizer, a barely controlled fireball named Victoria, had invited two other women to speak as well. Michelle George, an actress and singer, was a virtual legend in Canada for her spontaneous theatre work. She had been a member of Peter Brook's original company of actors, dancers, and musicians touring through the Middle East and Africa in the early 1970s. The third person, Oriah Mountain Dreamer, was a white woman who had been studying the ways of Native American Grandmothers and recently begun her own teaching program. Michelle, like me, had just turned fifty, and Oriah was in her mid-forties.

The organizer made us an unusual offer. We could choose any topic we liked, so long as it was about women and so long as we all participated, and she would create a conference for us. We scarcely knew each other but gamely agreed to meet and see if we could find some common ground. I flew in from California for a weekend, and we met at Oriah's apartment on Queen Street, next to the trolley car tracks. We sat around and drank coffee and told each other some of the stories of our lives. Eventually we tiptoed up to what we felt our edge was, the place where we needed to open spiritually to the matter that scared us most.

We all turned out to have the same edge. It's about getting old, we told each other. How did we feel about that? No, how did we really feel about that, apart from our fond ideas about Grandmothers of the Dreamtime and wise elders and how beautiful wrinkles are? We dove in, trying our best to be honest.

"Will I end up as a bag lady, standing alone on windy corners?" Michelle wondered.

I could see myself as the dotty spinster auntie, living in the third-floor attic of my niece's house, trying not to eat too much or draw anyone's notice. Someone, maybe Oriah, had an image of herself wearing polyester pantsuits and playing golf all day and canasta at night. And we all carried some version of living in a room in a nursing home, everyone we knew already dead.

Because these images were the scariest (we said "most challenging") we could think of, and because we were (bravely, crazily, grandiosely) determined to do something that hadn't been done before, we decided to create a conference about becoming elders. What does it mean to become a wise elder? We thought we'd ask that first. How can we become wise elders? That seemed like it could come next. What stands in our way? What support do we need?

We phoned Victoria in high spirits and announced that we had agreed on our topic: "The First Canadian Conference on Women Elders." She was thrilled. She liked the decisiveness of it, she told us, and would book a location in downtown Toronto right away.

As I look back, I tremble at what we were setting in motion that day. The stereotypes of aging we were carrying came from some mix of nineteenth-century novels, old movies, how we saw our grandparents aging, and the direst fears in our culture that equated growing old with becoming useless and dependent. Not that these fears weren't real concerns, but we were too young to be tackling them. We hadn't had enough direct experience to know which questions would open something genuine for the women coming to the conference and which would merely waste their time.

With twenty years of hindsight, I see how terrifyingly naïve we were about what was likely to happen when women in their midlife (us) tried to create a conference about elders. We had such warm feelings about how we'd bring together women of all ages. We'd help each other tackle the big questions, share our discoveries as sisters and friends. How little we knew of the sleeping furies we were about to disturb!

* * *

About five months before the conference, we developed a set of themes we wanted the women to explore. Michelle put together a sparkling array of theatre exercises to spice up the days. Oriah was going to bring her great six-foot drum, and her young assistants would lead chants they'd learned from their work with the Grandmothers. We were excited. Victoria was certainly right, we told each other. We made a good team, and it was going to be fun to dive into these questions about aging together.

To open the conference, we invited Marion Woodman, a respected Jungian analyst who had been a mentor for many Canadian women, including Michelle and me. Marion agreed to open the conference on Friday evening but said that she didn't want to prepare a talk. I was to interview her and it would all be very free form. Marion had been my analyst and then a friend for several years when I lived in Toronto, and I was delighted to be given this job. I re-read all of her books—she'd written about seven at that point—and thought carefully about the questions I'd pose. Then, about four months before the conference, Marion phoned. She'd been diagnosed with ovarian cancer. Letters and phone calls flew back and forth among her hundreds of clients and friends. Prayers from countless others surrounded her as she went through surgery and radiation therapy.

A month before the conference, Marion called Michelle to say that she would still like to give our opening talk. She explained that she no longer wanted an interview format, but if I could ask a question or two to get things started, she would simply answer spontaneously. It might be a very short talk, she warned, but if we still wanted her, she'd be there. We want you, Michelle told her. We absolutely want you.

On opening night, Marion and I walked up to the stage. As we took our seats facing each other, she smiled at me, and I tried not to cry. She was wearing a loose white pantsuit which did not do much to conceal the fact that she had lost about fifty pounds. Something happened first I think, some music. I stood to introduce Marion and talk about how she was showing the way as a truth teller we had not heard before.[1] Everyone knew about Marion's cancer, and the welcoming applause was thunderous. Marion nodded to me. I hadn't been able to think of a question so I waited for one to come. It was very simple.

"After all you've been through this year, Marion, what's it like to be here with us tonight?"

The oddest thing happened. Marion got up a little shakily and just stood for a while, getting her bearings. The stage lights seemed to brighten several orders of magnitude, and I could swear I saw her calmly unzipping her white pantsuit and letting it fall to the floor. And then she was slipping off her flesh and stepping out of that too, letting it fall to the floor. Then she was only light, radiant and silent. At some point I remembered to sit down and Marion started talking. I know that she seemed to gather strength as she went on, but I had no memory whatsoever of her words. At the end, she seemed somehow to have slipped back into her skin and pantsuit and taken her seat. The applause went on forever. In the midst of it and for some time afterward, a vast silence enfolded us.

Until You Are Naked

If I'd had the tiniest smidgen of humility or been able to register the quaking in the core of my body that night, I might have read the message. I think it was written in gold letters about thirty-feet high, echoing the Sumerian goddess Inanna in her descent to the Underworld: "Until you are naked, you cannot enter here."

Maybe it was written in Sumerian because not one of the three of us got the message that night. By Saturday morning, however, its wisdom was delivered with a flourish. My old friend Joan, the one who had laid in the Queen Anne's Lace with me twenty years earlier and taught me about pentimento, was the messenger. After Oriah and her young assistants opened the day with drumming and chanting and I had introduced the themes for the conference, I asked for comments from the audience. That's when Joan stood up.

She was sitting in the front row as my guest. In her seventies by then, Joan had become a professional storyteller and author. She had begun to carry a stout walking stick as tall as she was to assist her in on Toronto's icy streets. She had the stick with her that morning. Smacking it smartly against the floorboards, she shouted toward the stage, "What are you three doing up there? You're not elders! You don't have a grey hair on your heads." She turned and faced the shocked audience.

"Look! Where are the grey hairs? Where are the white hairs? We're down here, in the audience. We should be sitting up there, and they should be sitting down here, listening to us!"

A shudder of excitement undulated through the hundreds of women who were being addressed. I felt scared but somewhere inside I was rocking with laughter, shouting back, "Joan! You are so outrageous! You're here for free, and you're already disrupting the conference because you're not the center of attention."

The audience had turned toward me now, as had Joan, who had placed one hand on her hip, stuck out her belly, and was looking immensely pleased with herself. "Okay," I said. "You have a good point. Let's all take a break, and Michelle and Oriah and I will talk this over."

The women filed out for the toilets and tea in the outer hall, whispering, murmuring and apparently thrilled at the promise of a confrontation. The three of us huddled at the back of the stage, trying to decide what to do. It was clear that we needed to open the conference up right away and hear from some women besides Joan. But we had to admit that she had named the big bald thing that worried us most about the conference. We were not elders. "But we never said we were," we wailed. Well, too bad. Joan had poked her stick into what looked like it was going to be a very angry hornets' nest, and we needed to hear what the hornets had to say.

When the women returned, the first three or four were furious...at Joan. "We didn't drive all the way to Toronto to listen to a bunch of women we never heard of spout off their opinions," a woman with a strong northern Ontario accent declared.

"Sit down!" another shouted at Joan.

This was extraordinary, very un-Canadian behavior indeed. A number of women looked appalled, leaning over to comment to their neighbors with wrinkled brows and what I took to be sharp disapproval at the rude brouhaha. Then a few of the elders began politely to offer their opinions.

"I do think we should have a voice too," a thin woman with a perfectly white head of hair ventured.

Then it all seemed to break open. "We've paid good money," one exasperated voice called out, "and we don't intend to sit through a bloody debate for two days."

"Just get on with it, will you!" shouted another.

But there was no getting on with it. After considerably more back and forth, accompanied by increasing heat, Michelle announced that we would open the program for everyone who considered herself to be an elder (that solved the who was and who wasn't problem, we decided). "This evening, all of you who wish to can take the stage, and if you'll sit in a semi-circle, you can speak and respond to questions from the younger women."

Joan leapt to her feet. "That's too late," she announced. "We'll be tired by then. We need to speak in the afternoon." She was facing the roomful of women, not us, the so-called leaders. She reminded me of a painting of Saint Sophia I saw once, riding a white steed through a flaming sky above St. Petersburg.

"Totally in her element," I whispered to Michelle, who grinned back at me.

We agreed to change the time, and with our program agenda in utter shambles, proceeded. Michelle, a genius of improvisation, did what was probably the only thing we could have done at that point. She led the several hundred Canadian matrons in shouting, stamping their feet, and roaring out their feelings, all the feelings that were coming up now and had been coming up from what seemed to be beginningless time, getting suppressed and patted down and talked over. The church was rocking with the pure sounds of rage and tears and words that seemed to tear themselves through the women's bodies. Later, when there was time for sharing, some said they had never felt so much power pour through them. Others were frightened, bewildered, ecstatic. Finally, blessedly, it was time for lunch.

Meeting the Enemy

Michelle and Oriah and I made our way to my friend Ann's house, about a block away. Ann was in her sixties, midway between Joan and me, and the three of us had been friends for decades. Over hot soup and sandwiches, Ann talked about what had happened. She was mothering and grandmothering us, and we felt immensely grateful. We slurped our soup and worried out loud. We thought this conference would be about women coming together, we told her, and that we'd be helping everyone to reflect on genuine questions about getting old.

"You want to know what's coming up that you haven't heard yet?" Ann asked.

We groaned. There's more?

Ann looked at Oriah. "Imagine how you look to them," she said, "to the fat old ladies like me who are sitting in the back of the church."

We all looked at Oriah. She was slim, wearing a form-fitting dress with a big leather belt that curved in to show her tiny waist. Her beaded earrings sparkled through her long, perfectly coiffed blonde hair. She may have been pushing fifty but she didn't look it. She looked like a movie star.

"Women like you stole their husbands," Ann said. And she turned to Michelle and me, "And just because you two have a few grey hairs and are packing some extra pounds, you're not immune either."

She paused and spoke the next phrase slowly, making sure she had our attention, enunciating her words. "You are the enemy. You are the young wives who replace the old wives. You are the ones they used to be and aren't anymore. Your energy makes them feel tired. Your smooth faces accentuate their wrinkles. This stuff has been shoved under the rug for generations, for centuries. Old women are supposed to love young women, supposed to gracefully give up and let go of all they used to be and have and let that pass on to the ones who are coming after them. You want to be their sisters and their friends. Well, there's a lot of fury and grief and helplessness that has to get opened up before that has a prayer of happening!"

Over the next day and a half, every plan we made was in shreds within about five minutes. All we could do was to go in as naked as Marion Woodman had been on Friday night. Nobody knew what would happen next. Everyone was on the edge of their seats. Most of the women seemed to love it. Some said it was the most transformative, true experience of their lives. Some hated it and left shaken and disturbed.

On Sunday afternoon, the three of us sat together reflecting on the conference. "In case you're wondering where I am," Oriah said, "as I was coming downstairs for breakfast this morning, I found myself wishing I would fall and break a leg so I wouldn't have to show up today."

Michelle was alternately serene and laughing uproariously, leading all of us into the next big drama that ignited. Afterward she'd tell Oriah and me, "It was chaotic like this when our theatre company was improvising in Mali," and "It was like this when we were in Iran, inventing a new language."

"This is it," she'd say, "this is how it feels to be wide open, wild and free and right at the edge of the falls. Anything can happen and all you can do is be here for it."

As for me, the conference made me think of what Ann told me once about how she sailed across the Atlantic in a thirty-six-foot sloop. The year Ann turned sixty, she and her husband Sven set out in May, too late as it turned out to miss the catastrophic rogue storms no one had predicted. For endless days and nights, their boat was sucked up the arc of forty-foot waves and slammed down into the troughs, slashed with the force of tons of water washing across their bow. From moment to moment, they had no idea whether they'd make it through or drown.

Although we were sitting in a church in downtown Toronto, I had no doubt that The First Canadian Conference on Women Elders was doing that too—riding into massive waves and being slammed with towering forces. The hundreds of us gathered in those old pews were like our ancestors clinging to the railings of ships sailing to the new world—pioneers. Facing into centuries, maybe millennia, of lies and envy and fear that kept women across generations from trusting one another. I hoped that we were breaking new ground, but I didn't know if that was a delusion. All I knew was that we were riding the chaotic energies together, learning to tell and to hear hard truths. It was terrifying and exhilarating and there was no place I'd rather be.

As I look back, I think that the energies were so immense because so many of us were looking into the truth together. We needed the numbers. Penetrating our culture's shadow about aging is not something to be done alone.

Chapter 9

Unfolding the Questions

Always we want to learn from outside,
from absorbing other people's knowledge....
The trouble is that it's always other people's knowledge.
~Peter Kingsley,
In the Dark Places of Wisdom[1]

There was so much that we didn't know at that First Canadian Conference on Women Elders— almost everything, it seems as I look back. But there are two things I think we had right: we knew that we had to ask some of the key questions about growing old, and we knew that we had to do that as a community. The problem was that my friends and I were not nearly seasoned enough to know what to ask. Because we hadn't lived into the questions ourselves, we were in no position to pose them for others. And of course it mattered that we looked like what in fact we were—too young to be standing up there in the first place. So now I'm old enough to ask the questions. I do know that. If you're reading this, you're probably old enough too. But do you know the next necessary thing?

You have to let the questions find you.

Find you. Because if you try to do it the other way, probing and poking and analyzing your poor mind to its wit's end to try to figure out the questions that need to be asked, you'll just end up where you started from. As Rifka, a wise elder created by playwright Naomi Newman, advises: *Don't pretend you know where you are going. Because if you know where you are going, that means you've been there and you're going to end up in exactly the same place!*[2]

By questions, I'm not talking about analysis where you try to think your way logically to a conclusion, nor about mere queries that can be settled with the click of a browser. The kind of questions we need now lead to our own truth. They don't even have to look like questions. A line from a song or a poem, something you overhear on the bus, a feeling that won't go away — any of these can become soul-level questions. In our time when so little is understood about true maturity, when the maps we have lead us to places we no longer wish to go, when the paths we want to walk are inherently mysterious, we need these soul-deep questions to guide us.

I have learned how to let my questions find me, and to trust their precision and the beauty of their unfolding. But it was not always so. For much of my life, like Rose in the story that follows, I tried to give my questions away.

Rose and the Wise Elder

Once, in a tiny village in Eastern Europe, there lived a baker named Rose. Each day when she awoke, Rose would hum a little tune for the pure delight of waking and being a baker of breads. But on the morning of her fiftieth birthday, she lay in bed, her brows knit in a small frown. "There's a question that won't go away," she said to her husband. And the next morning the same thing happened. And the next after that. Rose asked her husband if he knew the answer, but he said, no, he had no idea.

Next Rose asked her mother, and each of her four sisters and her father and her neighbors on either side. None of them had an answer either. So Rose put on her good shawl and wrapped up a big loaf of double-braided raisin challah and went to visit the Rebbe who lived across the river. The Rebbe couldn't answer either but he had an idea. "There is a Wise Elder who lives in Chelm," he said, naming a town seven days distant. "Maybe she can answer your question."

So Rose set out for Chelm to ask her question of the Elder. At night she slept in farmers' barns when she could, and under thickets when there was no other shelter. Some evenings at dusk Rose saw the shadows of brown bears moving across the hills and some nights she heard the howling of wolves and could not sleep. Finally, on the morning of the eighth day, Rose reached the market square. She approached a cheerful-looking fellow selling potatoes and asked where she could find the Wise Elder. "Oh, you cannot see the Elder this year," he said. "She is in retreat, contemplating the mysteries of the universe."

A crowd gathered around. "Return to your home," they advised. "Come back next year."

"Oh dear," she said, for she was canny. "I suppose I will have to do that. But before I go, I'd like to see where the Elder lives."

Someone pointed up the hill. "Halfway up, beyond the gooseberry bushes."

"And does she really see no one?" Rose persisted.

"No one at all. Even the boy who brings her dinner has to leave the basket at her doorstep."

Rose made her way up the steep hill until she came to a cottage hidden behind some straggly bushes. A young boy was bending down to leave a covered basket on the stoop. Rose ducked into the bushes and took off her pack. She waited as the boy rapped on the door three times, and then skipped away. Soon the cottage door opened and a hand darted out, pulling the basket inside. At the next instant, Rose hurled herself through the door, landing at the feet of an astonished elderly woman. "I'm so glad to be here," Rose said in a rush. "I've traveled so far to meet you." As fast as she could, Rose explained about waking every day to the question that would not go away and asked the Elder to kindly answer her question.

The old woman opened her right hand, pulled it back quickly and smacked Rose hard across her left cheek. Shocked, Rose tried again, speaking louder and articulating each word in case the Elder had trouble hearing. "I have walked seven days and slept on the ground for seven nights to ask you my question that will not go away!" And again she told the Elder her question, and asked for an answer. This time the old woman opened her left hand, smacked Rose sharply across her right cheek, and with a push, shoved Rose out the open door and slammed it shut.

Rose sat on the ground, furious enough to spit. Which she did, several times to either side. After some long time, she brushed herself off, picked up her pack and began to make her way down the hill, mumbling furiously to herself. "Who says that woman is a wise Elder? She's stupid. Stupid and cruel! Didn't I tell her how far I'd travelled" — when she nearly bumped into a young woman descending the hill ahead of her. The woman said good day and asked if something was wrong. Rose poured out her whole story, ending with the words, "The famous Elder of Chelm is stupid. An entirely stupid Elder!"

The woman invited Rose to her home to discuss the matter further. As she sympathetically poured some Schnapps into Rose's tea, she confided that she was a student of the Elder's. "I think I know why she slapped you," she offered.

Rose waited, still angry but curious too.

"She slapped you the first time because you assumed that questions had to have answers," the woman said. "And she slapped you the second time because you were willing to trade your precious question for somebody else's answer."[3]

* * *

I heard this story the year I turned forty-seven, and it embarrassed me. I was doing just what Rose had done and I knew it — trying to trade my precious questions for somebody else's answers. Looking all the time for someone, some teacher or friend or mentor, or something, some great book or teaching, to address the deepest questions of my soul.

I wonder if we all need to be scalded like I was or shocked like Rose — repeatedly — to stop searching outside ourselves for the truth. I don't know. Maybe it can happen just once, and gracefully, the scales drop away from our eyes as we turn steadily to confront our own questions. It definitely wasn't like that for me. If I didn't give my questions away, I couldn't imagine what I would do with them. It took a long time to notice my assumption that I had to *do* anything with my questions—solve, resolve, give away, or otherwise get rid of them. Not until later did I discover that questions could be something entirely different from problems that had to be solved. They could be navigational devices pointing toward true north, compass stars, if I could find out how to use them.

Befriending the Questions

Eventually I learned that I needed to befriend my questions. Not *use* them, because they are not inanimate objects like stars or compasses or GPS devices. Questions, after all, come from us, from our longing to understand something true about our lives. If we just want information, we can connect with a library feed. Maybe—rarely—we will go and see for ourselves: how glaciers look when they're calving; what it's like to be on the Platte River when Sandhill Cranes rise in their thousands; the way rain changes the light on Amsterdam's canals.

But when it comes to intimate knowing, we need to let our questions find their way to us.

It's a little hard to talk about this. It's personal, the way that having a friend is personal. To be receptive to your questions is like leaning in to listen when a friend talks to you about something that really matters to her. You open yourself. You don't have an agenda stuck away in your back pocket.

I hope it's evident that these kind of deep questions aren't likely to show up as fully formed sentences or wake us from a dream as Rose's did. Sometimes that happens, but more often questions are musings, wonderings, fears or sorrows or joys that arrive for no reason we can name. They may be vague and repeated inclinations toward or away from something we can't define. So we hurry past them, brushing them away like fruit flies around the pineapple. Rarely do we take the time to pause, settle down, and let ourselves be curious about anything, including, or maybe especially, our experience of growing old.

Two Necessary Things

In the years after I heard the story of Rose and the Wise Elder, I did find out how to make friends with my questions. But I didn't learn how they could guide me until I met a master explorer named A.H. Almaas.[4]

To access the guiding intelligence of your own questions, Almaas said, you need two things. The first necessary thing is a matter of mind. You have to recognize that you actually don't know what you want to know. I thought maybe I'd heard him wrong. Why would he bother to mention anything so obvious? But it turns out that most of us hate not knowing things that are important to us. It's embarrassing, frustrating even, and tends to make us feel helpless. So we fudge around and think hard and look things up and ask our friends and forget that we ever wanted to know in the first place. Basically, we do whatever we can to avoid just sitting down with the unknown.

The second necessary thing is a matter of heart. We need to feel how much we *want* to know what's true. This is critical. It's what Rilke was advising when he told a young poet to learn to love the questions. And it's what the great botanist and inventor George Washington Carver meant when he said that whatever you love opens its secrets to you. The longing is what turns you inside out until you find the sun and the moon and the stars inside, as philosopher Peter Kingsley put it.[5] Without it, you can just sit around not knowing and never come to the truth you're seeking. Longing is the fire that fuels the questioning.

And to return for a moment to the first necessary thing — not knowing is critical too. If we have only longing, our question has no space in which to open. It's like the story of the professor who went to visit a Zen master so he could learn about Zen. As the professor expounded grandly on the many things he had read about Zen, the master quietly served tea. He filled the visitor's cup, and as the professor kept expounding, the master kept on pouring until the scalding tea spilled all over the table and into the professor's lap.

"It's overfull!" the professor screamed. "Can't you see that no more will go in?"

"Just so," the master replied. "How can I show you Zen with your mind so full?"

The Geese Are Flying South

Old-growth redwoods drip outside the window, and in the distance, fog. A pack of barking dogs seems to be heading toward me. Where am I? Sitting up in bed, I pull the quilt around my shoulders against the damp and wait. Here it comes: the hills above Half Moon Bay. I spot the wild geese now—not dogs, I realize—calling to each other in low, harsh barks. They're moving in tight formation through the fog, heading...where? What month is this? I wait again, longer this time.

August. Late August. It must be the fall migration. The geese are flying south.

Why did I take so long to figure out the month? I've never gotten used to these West Coast seasons. Green means winter when the rains finally come, and golden hills mean summer when everything has dried out. We don't have four seasons here—just two: wet and dry. Makes it hard for a normal person from New Jersey to know what month it is.

A lick of fear flashes up. I've lived in California almost thirty years. How come it's so hard these days to get oriented when I'm in a new place? I reach out to balance myself, not sure of my ground. Is my mind eroding the way beaches give way over time, the ocean pulling them back into itself?

Until this moment, thoughts like these have been just little flurries of worry, eddies in the general flow of mind moments. Now, as I let the questions come clearly into my mind, my fear becomes conscious too. Well, okay. Let the fear have some space, one of my teachers used to say. Let it breathe.

I'm letting it breathe. The fear gets bigger. This used to scare me: you pay attention and it gets bigger, for God's sakes! Who wants that? But I've come to trust the process. This is just how it works: pay attention and whatever you're feeling shows up more clearly.

I settle down a little. The fear feels like a chilly, uninvited guest clutching hard at my heart as if he wants to be invited for dinner. I sigh and stop fighting so hard. The guest makes himself at home, sloppily leaving his icy stuff all through my midsection. Breathe, I remind myself.

After some time, I begin to wonder what's scaring me. My curiosity makes the chill spread out and then soften and warm to a watery kind of energy. As I stay with it, the water becomes a flow. Nice, delicious actually, this energy washing through my arms and hands, pouring itself down my spine and all through my body and then the space beyond my skin. I feel like a dried-out ravine finally getting her river back. Nowhere to go, nothing to do, and nothing to be scared about.

I wait again. It's not the usual kind of tapping-your-foot, bouncing-your-leg, drumming-your-fingers, hurry-up-and-happen waiting. This is more receptive, a welcoming that doesn't even think of going someplace else. What's more, I feel content. Just being here is a pleasure.

Almost always, when I feel my fear open up like this, something unexpected happens. On this morning, I barely can find words for the lovingkindness that washes through me, pouring sweet nectar into the cells of my body. I rest, feeling nourished. Gradually I notice that my familiar sense of self has shifted into a deep calm and stability. I feel sober and mature, steady as a mountain and at the same time quite spacious and relaxed. The sensibility is of one ancient and wise.

All of this is quite paradoxical. I feel empty but it's not a hollow, something-is-terribly-lacking kind of emptiness. It is, rather, a sense of containing all possibilities—so unformed I'm no longer caught in my yesterdays; so free I'm miles of sky with no clouds.

Will I ever get over how experience changes when I don't run away from it? Here my fears about getting old and losing my mind have opened to a sense of maturity beyond anything I've known. And then there's that ancient, calm wisdom. How curious! Is this the perspective of an elder, I wonder? Can it unfold for anyone who questions their fears about growing old?

Birthing Each Other

Soul, psyche, the inner life, consciousness—whatever name you want to use—matures when we meet our experience with care and genuine curiosity. And although we can explore and inquire alone, a safe environment helps immensely.

"There's no scaffolding, no blueprint for becoming an elder today," my friend Marilyn insisted around the time she turned sixty-five. "Those of us who are past sixty have a tremendous spirit. But we don't know what form to give it. It's as if we're each in our own cocoon, unable to see what is unfolding. We're in the process of birthing the membrane that holds the new elder. We're going through for the first time, making our way toward a new way of aging most of us have never seen before.

"We need to be willing not to know what this will look like," she said. "To be open and to ask questions. Underneath the glitz of ads for houses on golf courses and happy white-haired couples in tennis clothes lies the terror of the grave," she told me, her voice trembling a little. "Become elders? Keep on maturing into old age? Forget it! We feel like failures, like dummies. If we had only taken more vitamins or exercised more or spent less time in the sun or not eaten red meat, then we'd still be resilient and strong and wrinkle-free, and most importantly, young."

She was furious at the lack of honest support from the culture. "All that junk we're inundated with about youth, pep, productivity, all the adulation of power and wealth... How do you find the courage to face the decline in your ability to function, to be honest with yourself about the memory failures, the trouble hearing, the fact that you can't earn what you once could? It's the anticipation of helplessness and uselessness that is so terrifying, and who wants to talk about that?"[6]

I was captivated. I wrote down what she said as best as I could and carried her words in my wallet, pulling them out from time to time to think about them. "We need to be elders for each other," she'd said. "We're birthing something new and we can't do it without support." And she'd used the word *courage*. It's a word I hear often from elders. I agree, of course. This time of our lives is definitely not for sissies. But to trust what is ripening in us now, we need something else too. We need each other.

We need to be honest mirrors for each other, because it's hard to trust what is developing in us when it is so different from what our mainstream culture values. Mother Culture, after all, is the default holding environment. She defines the game: what is normal, how to behave and how not to, what has meaning, and what is not worth bothering about. So long as we stay neatly inside her web, our familiar sense of self feels...well, familiar. Safe enough. We know our place in the world. We don't stick our necks out. We don't dive into the soul-deep questions.

Invisible Arms

As I've been musing on this matter of honest mirrors and genuine support, my thoughts keep turning to the social movements that began in the 1960s and '70s. They set off massive upheavals, changing the conventional worldview and the values of tens of millions of people. The most successful of these movements had two arms: a visible outreach with in-your-face public sit-ins and marches in the streets, and an invisible, hidden arm.[7] The public arms of the movements got the media coverage; the invisible ones happened in church basements and people's kitchens, and nobody outside took much notice of them at first.

Something about the hidden parts of those movements kept buzzing around in my mind, pestering me to pay attention. I finally went down to the garage. Pushing past too many suitcases and boxes of tax receipts back to 1996, I found what I was looking for—Mary Daly's *Gyn/ecology* with its description of the invisible arm of the women's movement.

"In concealed workshops, spinsters unsnarl, unknot, untie, unweave," she writes. "We knit, knot, interlace, entwine, whirl and twirl..." mending a consciousness that has been split against itself, that has focused only on externals. And what women found, she said, was a place to develop their integrity and ways to break the spell of the culture's clocks.[8]

So I've been wondering: can we, too, unsnarl and unweave the web of beliefs and stories about what it means to grow old? Can we break the spell of life's morning to find the integrity of life's evening? I look for clues from the modest, invisible arms of the women's circles that met outside of the public eye.

One of the most important clues: the "spinsters" didn't try to do it alone. They met together. A lot of us remember how hard it was, and awkward, trying to talk to each other. Hard work we weren't good at, and yet we knew that we needed each other. As one of my friends put it then, "To find my own truth, I need to know not just that someone will put up with what I have to say. I need to feel that they actually want to hear me."

We all want that: to be welcomed into finding our truth and our expression. It was what theologian Nelle Morton meant when she said we were hearing each other into speech. I take this to be a second clue: we need to listen carefully to one another, not only with kindness but with genuine interest.

And one more thing seems important: I think we need to meet with other elders. The matters before us now are often hard to articulate and easy to mistake. Some seem to be untranslatable. But if we will take the time and delve together into what is unfolding in us, what is unfolding can ripen. With each other for companionship, we might recognize ourselves as the growing tip of being human, in the process of bearing new kinds of fruit.

Asking the Questions Together

When I was rooting around in the garage trying to find Mary Daly's book on the women's movement, I came across a skinny purple pamphlet by Mary Morrison, a Quaker gospel studies teacher I'd met in Philadelphia decades ago. I sat down on the step to see what Mary had to say. "These writings are my reflections on aging," she wrote, "for which I am qualified, if by nothing else than having reached the age of 83." I smiled, remembering her brisk, no-nonsense manner.

Then, rather abruptly, she announced what she considered to be the question of ultimate importance in growing old: "How are we going to respond to the inevitable and growing diminishment that is coming upon us?"

Oh God. Diminishment. I tried the word out on my tongue. Ugh. Who even heard of that word before? Something like deficiency but worse. It stuck to me, or in me, like a prickly burr, as did its assertion of relentless decline. Just as I was thinking it was time to dump the pamphlet and make myself a tuna-fish sandwich, one line grabbed my attention. "To be able to address this question," Mary wrote, would call on "the quiet and patient gallantry, the heroism, to find the Elder in ourselves."

I'm sure I groaned. She'd hooked me. Over the next couple of days the word "diminishment" took up residence in my mind and showed no sign of moving on. I was not exactly curious about my inevitable diminishment, as Mary so insistently named it. I just couldn't get rid of the question. So I decided to bring it to the new elders' group I was starting with my friend David (in a church basement in Berkeley, as you might have guessed). When I brought up Mary's awful word, I swear I could feel seventy bellies clenching in unison. I rolled my eyes at David in a silent—"Forgive me!"—and went on talking about why it might be worth exploring what this word brought up. After a while, I noticed some curiosity edging into the space. Eventually I gave them Mary's question to work with in small groups, using a slightly different form: "How are you going to respond to the inevitable and growing diminishment that is or will be coming into your life?"

As David and I sat watching from the side of the room, it seemed to me that the elders were biting into the question, pulling it apart, and tearing into its flesh. I suppose that is a tad dramatic. I was no doubt projecting my own fears onto the group. Diminishment was certainly worrying David and me as well. That's why we had decided to do the group in the first place—to grapple with some of the swarm of things that scared us about getting old. In any case, tearing into the question was exactly what the elders ended up doing. They were yanking it apart like a carcass thrown to a pack of starving coyotes. (A deer carcass, in case you were wondering.)

The question of diminishment turned them on, they told us later. It was the stinky stuff under the rug, the shadow under the shiny just-fine-thanks patina that they were sick of living with. Here, with the strength of their numbers and the structure of a question naming the fear, the elders were ferocious. A redhead in a rhinestone-studded pantsuit stood up. "Of course we're going through losses," she said. "And deaths. And weakness and fear for the future. If we don't look at the hard questions and cultivate our inner support, we'll fall on our faces." She took her time looking around the room, making sure everyone had heard her.

A white-haired poet in a flannel shirt stood up next. Waiting until the room was completely quiet, he said, "I want to find out how not to lie to myself as I grow older." Several heads nodded.

A physicist who said he had come only to humor his wife, announced, "I want to know how to open up this whole aging thing—the full catastrophe—all the stuff I can't do any longer but also the wisdom or compassion or anything else that can develop in me now."

David and I grinned at each other. This seemed to be going well, all these insightful, honest comments. Someone else spoke about what it was like to "preside over the disintegration of your own body."

Another talked about watching that kind of process take place in her husband, "losing my friend," she said, to Alzheimer's. As the sharing deepened, becoming more vulnerable and naming some of the most painful experiences of aging, I started to feel sleepy. Soon, embarrassing, head-rolling grogginess was overcoming me. It seemed to be seeping through the cracks in the windows like greasy gray fog, but I knew it wasn't coming from the outside. I could feel the group's curiosity about diminishment evaporating by the minute. David leaned over to me and whispered one word: **Denial**. I sighed.

After lunch, we decided that we had better get the denial out in the open. We asked the elders to sit facing a partner and ask a question we would give them. Each time their partner replied, they were to ask the question again. After fifteen minutes they would switch places and ask a second question in the same way. Everyone looked pretty perky and ready to write down the questions.

David said, "Here's the first one: 'Tell me a way you deny your experience of diminishment.' Wait till both of you have answered that question and then do the second one: 'What's it like to feel the denial now?'"

Loud moans and groans and bursts of laughter followed, accompanied by the scraping of chairs as the elders gamely paired up and plunged into their inquiries. David and I speed-walked the hill to the rose gardens to wake ourselves up. By the time we returned an hour later, it seemed like a lightning storm had blown through, clearing every trace of fog. Evidently the questions about denial had an effect. The elders were immensely pleased with what they discovered, and several of them announced that they were eager to return to future groups for more such questions.

On the drive home, I was feeling happy with the day until it occurred to me that I hadn't addressed Mary's question myself. I decided I'd better plunge in right after dinner with my favorite collaborator in denial, my husband Paul. He'd made grilled salmon and his special zucchini parmesan, and as we ate I alternately wheedled and waxed enthusiastic about how interesting it would be to explore our fears about diminishment. Amazingly, he agreed. But once we had washed the dishes and sat down in the living room, I began to yawn. Big, noisy, open-mouthed yawns just seemed to roll out, one after another.

"Tired, Babe?" Paul asked sympathetically. "Maybe we should leave it for another day."

But I knew exactly what was going on. "Let's just do it," I said.

We dived in, and it wasn't easy. I wished that we were in that church basement with seventy companions because I definitely didn't feel like a pack of coyotes tackling that question, and neither did Paul. More like swamp sludge. But finally we opened up some of our fears and got to the denial questions. Like magic, my grogginess disappeared. And we both brightened, relieved to feel the clarity and actually be interested in the truth of what we'd been avoiding for way too long.

What impressed me most from that day was how powerful it was to be able to ask those hard questions together. Of course, the questions themselves would have had no strength without the elders' determination to get to the truth that mattered to them.

PART IV

RIPENESS

...And people will untie themselves, as string is unknotted,
Unfold and yawn and stretch and spread their fingers,
Unfurl, uncurl like seaweed returned to the sea....

And the clocks will stop, and no one will wonder or care or
notice,

And people will smile without reason, even in winter, even in
the rain.

~ A. S. J. Tessimond, *Day Dream*[1]

We will untie ourselves, the poet says. Unfold and yawn and stretch...doesn't that sound lovely? Oh, now is definitely the time for this, don't you think? This must be what it means to grow ripe, when the earnest do-gooders and noble get-it-righters and hurried go-fers in our psyche stop taking themselves so seriously and sit down and put up their tired feet. Something really does unfold when we let ourselves be. All manner of things, actually. Weariness—that we've been pushing away for too long. Jumbles of thoughts that have been entangling us. Quiet arises naturally—patches of genuine silence. And when we let ourselves be as we are, what we are becomes known to us.

Last July, I had a delicious taste of the ripeness that develops when someone lets the clock stop. In celebration of a friend's birthday, I suggested that a few of us drive up to the wine country to see the work of an artist named Marie Ali. It was a little hard convincing everyone that this would be a good idea once I mentioned that the art we'd be driving two hours to see was quilt-making. I think my friend Harry may have groaned slightly. As a writer who has published books on art and beauty, he let me know that he had his standards and...quilts? Well, he was dubious.

I said, more sharply than necessary, that he couldn't imagine the exquisite, wild mystery of Marie's work and that he should just come along and see for himself. He smiled and agreed good-naturedly. The following weekend five of us drove through the dusty purples of Sonoma's vineyards to the winery where the quilts were on display. We toured through the rooms, awed by the vast hangings showing galaxies and rainforests and abstract wonders I won't even try to describe. When we settled down afterward for some wine-tasting, Marie came by to say hello. Harry seemed particularly fascinated.

"Did you ever make the usual kind of patchwork quilts?" he quizzed her.

"Oh yes," she said, "for many years."

"Well, what made you change and start crafting these extraordinary works of art?"

Marie thought for a moment. "When I stopped caring how long it took," she said.

For most of human history, as I mentioned earlier, we've had long springtimes and the shortest of summers—a lot of years to put down roots and almost none to bear fruit. But our longevity has leapt ahead in the last century, giving our species ripening time like never before. We're living in this period now. If we are graced with good health and a reasonably safe environment, if we extricate ourselves (at least somewhat) from the cultural and personal obstacles in our way, we can ripen. We can cultivate what is developing naturally and mature.

Well maybe, you might be thinking. But how can we tell when we're ripe?

We can tell from the inside, it seems to me. We notice that we've relaxed, untied and untangled ourselves. We let go of the dizzy belief that we are the center of the universe and must have an impact on everything around us. And we feel pleasure for no reason, or for every reason—for the sharp needles of rain pelting our window this night, or because a guy named James who looks like a linebacker and is supposed to be selling us an iPhone at AT&T stops the sales pitch to pull out a picture of his baby girl and beam like he'd swallowed the sun. Or a hundred other things that let us know what grace it is simply to be here, in the life that we are given, in the time that we have left.

On the other hand, we're not apples. All you need to do is bite into a Granny Smith. If it's crisp and firm, it's ripe. Gravensteins get sweet and tart and kind of tender. If you know the fruit, you can tell when it has come to full flavor. With us, it's more complicated. We're a new fruit, or at least a new development in an old variety. Our mature flavors are not fully known. However, in this final section, we'll explore some of the possibilities.

Chapter 10

Becoming an Elder

For those who embrace the gifts reserved for age...
old age becomes freedom,
becomes the dance....
~Helen Luke, *Old Age*[1]

Have you noticed that we give two different meanings to the word elder? A clue is the use of a capital letter. If you are an *Elder*, you're a valued member of the community. If you're an *elder*, you're just old, with all the connotations of what I called earlier "That Aging Thing" where so much is coated with slick and unappealing connotations of being out of date, irrelevant and invisible.

But there can also be an "Elders Thing." It's just as coated with meanings, but now the clingy stuff is grand. Add that capital *E* and you're dignified, wise and possibly somewhat saintly. Elder or elder—both loaded with projections. So long as we buy into them, we're hapless flies trapped in Mother Culture's web. Still, when you dig underneath the projections, you always find something. What we find with "elder/Elder" is, I think, a longing for something real, something we recognize in certain elders. It might be a depth of humanity or some quality of kindness or generosity that evokes our longing to live that in ourselves.

As I look at it, an elder—let's drop that capital E and I'll try to make the meaning clear from the context—is more of a verb rather than a noun, to borrow from Buckminster Fuller. Or actually, it's more of gerund—more a way of being than doing; a way of engaging and perceiving and being with yourself and others but not a role. Not a job description. So no one who is an elder needs to act like an elder all the time. You can be a person of no age, like Harpo Marx. Or you can be sixteen years old, dancing your heart out. Or, as the eminent Jungian analyst Helen Luke wrote in her eighties, you can be freedom, the dance itself.

Trying to be an Elder

Still, it's so normal to *try* to be an elder. When the writer Michael Meade was in his early fifties, he asked a question that I thought was splendid: *How do I find the courage to let the hero die so the elder can be born?* I loved him for asking that, the vulnerability of it, coming from a guy who had spent his life being tough, cynical, and keeping it all together.

But it's a middle-aged question. When I met Michael at a conference in Northern California, I was in my fifties too, and that's what I wanted—to become an elder. I thought it was something I had to do.

Trying to be an elder is the perspective from the outside. It's the grand view, where "elder" has an impressive and baffling mystique and a story that reads like an encyclopedia. A set of encyclopedias, actually. My personal library, casually put together over the last thirty years, runs to fifty volumes without even trying: *Wisdom of the Elders. Ageless Elders. How to be a Christian Elder, Jewish Elder, Planetary Elder. Spiritual Practices for Elders. Native American Life Stories of Elders with Photographs. Wise Women Elders. Elders of the Dreamtime.* And so on. The tower of concepts must reach to the high heavens, so much earnest effort has been expended on describing how to become one of these paragons.

There's obviously a gap here. When people who are old enough to be elders encounter the idealized outside viewpoint, they're pretty sure they aren't and probably never will be an Elder. How do we make sense of this?

I think it's a matter of what the people I've worked with call "the hard stuff." The stuff that life brings if you live long enough to grow old—the losses and endings that nobody wants but everybody gets. Helen Luke has a more elegant term. She calls these events and the life experiences they catalyze "the gifts reserved for age."[2]

The Gifts Reserved for Age

It's a strange to call something a gift when no one wants it. My short and not exhaustive list of the strange gifts that come as we age includes: fury at the cruelty and ignorance we see in the world; helplessness to erase that; regret for the suffering we've caused; fear of our own suffering, hidden in memories; grief for beloveds we have lost to dementia and death; anticipation of our own death.

These experiences, and the unraveling and vulnerability they can bring feel like earthquakes. They feel like tornados, hurricanes, avalanches—catastrophes of nature. Maybe not always, not totally, but gifts? How can endings and suffering lead human being into maturity? All *gifts*, Luke insists, because being present to these experiences transforms us.

And don't forget death, she says. If you leave out death, you cannot become a true elder for your people.

Including Death

Few days go by that I'm not aware of the nearness of death. It has begun to feel normal. Small calculations about the time remaining run in the back of my mind. I read the obituaries in *The New York Times* for people I've never met. I get something from this. It's not grisly the way I used to think it was when my grandparents did it. Something else—maybe I feel called to bear witness to the full span of a person's life and how they filled it. A call came yesterday from a close friend about the death of her sister. Another friend died last week in the midst of her bath. I reach out in bed to touch Paul when he stops snoring, to see if he's still alive. He does the same with me. "Unmediated," he tells me, the raw fear that comes in the middle of the night, half asleep, when he can't hear me breathing.

"Do you check on me often," I ask him.

"No, not often," he says. "But sometimes."

Death has begun to feel like a continual murmur, an intimate consultation I do with the end point that is coming. It's not something I talk about, but a kind of certainty is here now, making this time distinctly different from my middle age.

Earlier I talked about how many aspects of aging are new to our era. But the need to be aware of our death is not new. It's one of the key spiritual and philosophical insights about our existence, the crucial choice that turns human beings toward maturity. Toward, in the words of Psalm 90, a heart of wisdom.

The 3,500-year-old Sumerian myth of Inanna is one of the oldest teaching stories to point this out. I first encountered the dramatic tale in the poem cycle recounted by Diane Wolkstein and Samuel Noah Kramer. At the point that's important for us here, the Queen of Heaven and Earth "set her ear to the Great Below." What she heard, the story says, is the sound of her long-lost sister weeping. The action unfolds dramatically after this, telling how Inanna closed every one of her temples and prepared to descend to the underworld; how she arrayed herself first in the symbols of her power and then, in her descent, was forced to remove every one; and how, naked, she entered the last gate and was brought to the other half of herself, the sister who sat grieving in the dry, dark realm of the Great Unknown; and ultimately, how Inanna dies and is reborn.

But two things are not told in this account. What made Inanna listen so carefully before there was any sound? And why didn't she turn back when the guardians at the gates demanded that she give up her crown, her lapis rod and staff of authority, her breastplate, and the golden sandals?

We are not told because it was obvious, I presume. The people of that time would have understood the poem cycle as a wisdom teaching describing the course of a fulfilled life. They would

have known that Inanna made the only choice she could make—
to turn from the triumphs of her youth and middle years to
descend toward the unknown, toward the place most feared, to
meet her death. So everyone would understand that birth and
death, life and death, could not split apart but must be known in
their wholeness.

And just in case the wisdom of Inanna's choice was not crystal
clear, her story is immediately followed in the poem cycle by that
of Dumuzi, her husband. When the demons of the underworld
arrive for the king, he frantically runs and hides, desperate to
hold on to his kingship, his royal throne, his freedom. Eventually,
of course, Dumuzi is caught. Trapped by the demons, he
persuades his sister to share his burden. Thus, forever after that,
Dumuzi returns to the upper world for half the year and then
must die again and return to the underworld. That's how it is, the
wisdom story tells us, for those who try to escape reality: death
after death after death.[3]

Initiates All

Traditional societies and the mystery cults of Greece and Rome
taught the same basic wisdom story as the Inanna-Dumuzi myth.
Through transformational rites of passage, they carried their
people into encounters with death and rebirth. Initiates were
separated, often isolated, from their former way of life, and their
familiar identities were stripped away. Sometimes this meant
days in darkness. At other times and other places, the initiate
spent weeks fasting in solitude in the desert, staying in one
location or walking continuously. Open as the sky to all that
would or would not come. Watching through the long nights as
the stars wheeled through the blackness. Emptying out who they
thought they were, as the elders sat far away in their circle,
praying for the ones in the fertile void. Even when the ones in the
threshold forgot, believing themselves alone and lost, the elders
prayed. When the time was complete, the initiates returned to

their people, and the period of the integration would begin.

A Caribou Eskimo shaman, describing his experience, recalled: "I died a number of times during those thirty days but I learned and found what can be found and learned only in the silence, away from the multitude, in the depths. I heard the voice of nature itself speak to me, and it spoke with the voice of a gentle motherly solicitude and affection. Or it sounded sometimes like children's voices, or sometimes like falling snow, and what it said was, 'Do not be afraid of the universe.'"[4]

Rites of passage were designed to bring the initiates to this point of complete internal security. So that when they did return, they would know, with an unshakable certainty, the wholeness of all life in which they were absolutely included.[5] We no longer have full rites of passage as an inheritance from our ancestors. And most of us no longer have elders in this world who sit in their circles, praying us through the cycles of separation, initiation, and return. But this is not to say that we no longer travel those searing and lonely passages because aging makes initiates of us all. Without formal rituals or circles praying for us, without a way prepared but moving nevertheless, we proceed not knowing—for who can truly know—what death will bring? We are guaranteed only an ending to the life we have known. If we let the nearness of this ending impact and open us, we no longer live on the surface of life. We enter and move into the depth.

The gifts reserved for age bring us belly to belly, heart to heart, with the experiences that can mature us. They are gifts because they make us long for the dark places of wisdom and meaning in life;[6] and because they open the way for us to mature into our promise as human beings.

We can refuse these strange gifts, reject them. My mother refused them as much as she could. "Don't tell me," she'd say. "I don't want to know." She was eleven when the Great Depression hit. Her friends' fathers were jumping out of windows. "It's best not to know," she'd tell me. "We have to move on."

Or we can open to our experience, set our ear to the Great Unknown and listen. When the time is right—or when it isn't right at all but we have to anyway—we can turn toward what comes to meet us and engage with it as best we can. Who's to judge such choices? Through grace or luck or some miracle of willingness, we may be able to let the strange gifts unfold us. Or, for lack of support and resources, we may get halfway through and stop. I don't think it's an either-or. At any time, we're all probably somewhere in this cycle, like people in a labyrinth walking the winding path. Not knowing if we'll be carried directly to the space at the center or sent arcing to the distant outer edges, far from where we hoped to go.

Whatever the path, at some point we come to the threshold where our death is waiting.

Endings

For many years I worked as a psychotherapist in an office that had little to recommend it except for an excellent view of a black oak tree in the yard next door. Between my therapy clients, I would stand at the window, taking in the display of tender green parasols in springtime, and in winter, stark branches against a faded sky. The previous occupant had left a framed calligraphy next to the window. When I wasn't looking at the tree, I'd sometimes read the calligraphy:

I know this cup is already broken so I enjoy it completely.

I'd think about the writer turning his cup, a little stained perhaps around the swirl of its neck, a soft glimmer of light along its lip. And I'd gaze at the tree, admiring its leafy shadows bobbing across my room, knowing that the November rains would knock those leaves to the ground and the cold would wither them. I thought about how endings make everything precious. It was an idea then, something to contemplate. That changes too, of course. The year I turned sixty-five, endings stopped being a concept.

On a Wednesday night in the middle of a busy week, I was trying to schedule a yoga retreat in between several teaching commitments when my doctor phoned. "How nice of you to call this late," I said, with what turned out to be stunning naivety. He announced briskly that the bruise on my arm he'd dismissed a year earlier biopsied as a melanoma. He'd scheduled surgery for Friday morning.

In a way, it's all so straightforward once you get a cancer diagnosis. You cancel everything. That first quick surgery was followed by another, and then another. With the cascade of tests and surgeries and downtime and cancelling and rescheduling, it wasn't until a fourth surgery was scheduled that it occurred to me to wonder how I felt about dying.

Letting the question of death surface was like throwing the brakes on a speeding train. Not violent but definitive. Ever since the diagnosis, even when I was standing still, I had been rushing on the inside, anxious about the surgeries and afraid of more pain. Once the question of death arrived, I stopped.

I took myself upstairs to settle into my blue rocking chair and wait. It took a while of rocking and looking out the window and not doing a blessed thing. Eventually, I found myself wondering what I would miss. So much felt complete: my work, the friendships that are dear to me, my love for Paul. I don't have children or grandchildren whom I hope to see grow up. There wasn't any sense of things left undone. I can go, I thought. I felt a kind of neutrality—dispassionate and at the same time, interested. My heart had utterly relaxed.

Really? So there's nothing to keep me here?

As I rested, that neutrality spread into what I would call, in retrospect, a sense of freedom. Unimpeded. No push toward death or pull toward life, nothing to do and nowhere to go. And then—it was a sudden thing—the pure goodness of Life itself flooded into my awareness. I would say that this was love but it was not a love I had ever known because it was not attached to anything at all. It was like love in that my heart was very glad and full, so happy to savor this goodness. And whether this was love or freedom or simply life, I knew then, with the deepest certainty, that I would like to live purely for life itself. All of it, just as it is: the orange cat killing a sparrow in my backyard, Paul in the kitchen cursing the coffee machine, and my arm with the scar needing more surgery. All perfect.

After my fourth surgery, there were no more signs of melanoma. I still go for check-ups, and I don't mind at all. They help to remind me to be grateful for my precious and impermanent life.

The Gift of Endings[7]

Not only our own death brings us to an awareness of endings, of course. As we age, we may become caregivers for our beloveds. Many elders I know are doing this kind of service, and some say that they are no longer afraid of death. I heard these words again last night from Pamela, a woman in her eighties who has been the main caregiver for her husband and sister, both of whom died recently from dementia.

As we sat in an elders' circle, Pamela spoke about what she had learned from spending most of each day for the past two years with people she loved dearly, as their minds disintegrated. They were in pain, she told us, not so much physically as emotionally, especially when they first understood what was happening to them. "But they also had such courage and...I'd have to say, grace, over those years. And for both of them, their dying was graceful..." Her voice trailed off and she sat for some time, seeming to consider whether what she had said was true. Eventually she looked around the circle. She was even more settled, resting in herself. "Graceful," she repeated quietly. "Some people might question that, but I know what I know."

I looked into what seemed to be a well of luminous night shining in her eyes. Lines from an Anatolian fairytale drifted to mind: *Night like the silent flight of black swans, carrying with them the silence...* That's how it felt last night, hearing Pamela speak: open, unbounded. A fine mystery embraced us all—the one who was lonely and the one who doubted she'd ever be an elder, and the youngest one, a man in his fifties who had spent more time with death than any of us.

* * *

"Each of us walks as honest a journey as we can," my friend Ann told me one night as we were communing long distance over Skype. "We all have different temperaments. An awful lot of people become frantically unhappy and then apathetic as they grow old."

She sounded rather gruff—a mixture of sorrow, I thought, and telling me the truth from her eighties. Then I realized that she was also remembering her decades as a social worker, visiting nursing homes and sitting with old people who lived alone or almost alone. "Not so many of us mature," she went on. "It's so important to contact the depth in ourselves while we still can, find our connection with the universal ground." She paused to see if her words were getting through. "I think this should go into that book of yours," she said emphatically. "People need to know."

Chapter 11

The Presence of Elders

Winters tend to be cold in Holland, with a chilling grey damp that seeps into your bones as you walk along the canals seeking a bit of sun. But the sun is hidden, coming mostly in glimmers off the dark waters. Those dreary winters make it easy to understand Dutch artists' preoccupation with light and the Dutch passion for their beloved tulips in spring. When I found out that cold is the tulip's ally, forcing the bulbs into vibrant bloom, it struck me as only fair—those startling purples and electric reds, yellows and oranges and pinks and impossible shining blacks showing up because of the long chill winters they've been through.

Each April, when I arrive in Amsterdam to teach, I fall in love with tulips all over again. In the past few years, as I peer into window boxes and stroll past the great round tulip beds of Vondelpark, I've found myself thinking about elders: how we, too, mature from hard winters, amazing as tulips sprouting from those raggedy, hairy bulbs. It's so unexpected that from the times when everything falls to pieces, when every part of you wants to turn away or run away, you come to know true things directly, intimately, miles below words and concepts. And it's so confounding to our ordinary ways of thinking that from such times, we can mature into elders with gifts to share.

The great gift that elders have to give is not what most people imagine. It doesn't look like the competencies we're proud of in our youth and middle age. It's not the impressive accomplishments admired in the media. Many times, the fruit of a life deeply lived is almost invisible, and elders themselves may not recognize it. But it has great value nevertheless. It is the gift of presence. With it, we can become mature elders for our people. Without it, we simply grow old.

You Don't Have to Try

One rainy afternoon last November, Paul and I drove through the drenched hills of West Marin to celebrate Thanksgiving with a few friends. Julia and Sandy had a fire going and with the darkness and the clattering rain against the windows and their big labrador dozing by the fire, there was a sense of comforting warmth. By the time the seven of us moved into the dining room, the intimacy had deepened. Our voices were low and we were listening to each other in a way you almost never do at holiday dinner tables.

Something happened after the turkey and Brussels sprouts and sweet potato pie, a very small thing perhaps, that has stayed with me. We'd already cleared the dishes for dessert when I had the impression that Sandy stood up at the far end of the table where he was sitting. I can't imagine that this is right, that Sandy would have called attention to himself like that. He's a quiet guy, a poet who writes about war and finding your way through the chaos, or maybe not finding it at all but writing about it anyway. Whether or not he stood up, we stopped talking and all turned toward him. He started to tell us about a meeting he'd been invited to with veterans from Iraq and Afghanistan.

"It's been forty years since I was a Marine in Vietnam," he said, and he wasn't sure he'd have anything to offer these young vets. "But after ridiculous amounts of coffee and a few hours of listening, I realized it was important that I was there." He took a sip of the not-very-good wine I'd brought and looked nowhere in particular, some place private. Nobody said anything.

"Maybe I was an elder for them," he reflected. "Maybe paying attention the way I did, asking a question sometimes, I was bringing something they needed. Because you see, they didn't know if they could live with what happened there."

Sandy looked around then as if he'd just noticed us. "You know," he broke into a half grin, "it's different from what I thought it would be, this elder thing. You don't have to try to do anything. They come to you."[1]

What Sandy didn't say but seemed obvious was that Vietnam counted. And that his years of working through what happened there—all that he could put into his poems and all that he hadn't written and maybe never would—counted even more. And what I would say is that you don't have to try to be an elder because your presence is the gift.

The Gift of Presence

Over the years I have heard many stories of elders spanning a chasm that seemed unbridgeable. Sandy Scull's link across forty years is one example. Another is the weave that a theologian named Ellie Haney created with other elders to keep a community from disintegrating. I'll tell you about that soon. And there are other stories about bearing witness, creating initiations and blessing ceremonies, expanding the perspective of a church, and making a space in a downtown bus station where people can talk to someone who will listen. As I reflect on these stories, I see what I suppose you could call two truths, or maybe, two levels of the same truth.

The first truth is the one I just described: the elders did such and such a thing and so we didn't fall apart, or we saw things differently, or we found a way to open our hearts. And the second truth is one that comes more gradually. Beneath the particular events that occur, mature elders bring a profoundly human quality that is sometimes called simply "presence."

Presence is rarely named and is a bit hard to describe.[2] It is a way of being wholeheartedly here. Its perception is inherent to our human consciousness, but has been pretty much been disavowed in public discourse since the so-called Enlightenment. Presence means, very approximately, showing up body and mind and spirit to whatever might be in store. When someone is present in this way, you can feel it. You feel that they're right there with you, and that something genuine is happening.

Sometimes the quality of presence feels loving or supportive and you say, I could feel his love, or I sensed her support even though she didn't say a thing. At other times presence is called 'bearing witness' and it doesn't feel like love or support, exactly, but still there is an awareness—substantial, immediate—of someone taking her seat in the circle, or standing for what he believes.

Being present is not a matter of doing, saying, solving, or resolving anything. It's freer than that. Behind whatever practical wisdom or long experience mature elders bring, whatever caregiving they do or generosity they show, whether they are actively advising or silent, the quality of presence seems to be essential. It's the underpinning, the *sine qua non*, that makes you feel simply being with this person is a gift.

The Presence of a Listener

In the seventies in San Francisco and New York and Toronto and dozens of other cities across North America and by the eighties in Western Europe and Israel as well, women gathered in groups to explore their experience of the sacred. In a very few places, these gatherings grew into thriving women's communities. In most others, the fledgling communities started with high hopes and faltered, dissolving in acrimony within a few years.

One of the shining exceptions to this disintegration was a gathering of three hundred women that called itself the Feminist Spiritual Community of Portland, Maine. About six years after the group began, Patricia Hopkins and I travelled to interview its founders and some of its members. We were most curious to discover how they had managed not to fall apart.

Ellie Haney, one of the founders, told us that the community started with a lot of heterogeneity. Everyone thought that was a good thing, until they didn't. After a summer of fights and arguments and anguished soul-searching, Ellie told us, the community agreed on a principle: 'In our diversity is our strength.'

Was that it? Pat and I knew too well how such principles could dissolve like landfill in an earthquake. We asked to talk to some of the long-time members. "It was the elders like Ellie who held us together," one woman explained. I asked what the elders told them to keep the community from splintering.

She seemed surprised at my question. "They didn't tell us anything."

"Well, what did they do?"

"They listened. When any one of us spoke, our elders paid attention with so much care that we finally started to listen to one another. That's all."

Her friend repeated, "That's what turned things around. They didn't take sides and they listened."

* * *

Centuries ago, women on the wild south coast of England would stand holding lanterns to guide their fishermen through storms. The presence of an elder can be like that: a beacon when the sailing is rough and the compass stars are hidden. Ellie was that kind of beacon for the women in Portland. When she died, her friends set up a foundation in her name. On the website, they praised what they called her "engagement." I don't imagine they meant advice giving because everyone talked about how good Ellie was at listening. "Listening" seems to be another name that people give to what I am calling presence: a way of being that opens the possibilities and inspires others to listen to themselves; a receptiveness that invites whatever is fresh and genuine in the speaker; an actual current you can feel if you pay attention.

A Magnetic Force

Who are the people to whom you go for advice? Not to the hard ones who can tell you exactly what to do, but to the listeners; that is, the

least censorious, least bossy people you know. It is because by pouring out your problem to them, you then know what to do about it yourself.
~Brenda Ueland, *Tell Me More*[4]

The writer Brenda Ueland was passionate about the power of what she called listening. A magnetic and strange thing happens, she said, a creative force "makes us unfold and expand. Ideas actually grow within us and come to life."

Brenda (I call her that; I can't imagine she would tolerate anything else) is one of my heroine elders whom I never got to meet. She was born in 1892 and lived to be ninety-three. She radiated presence even when she wasn't listening. Reading her books, you feel her leaping out to meet you and take your hand.

Whether you call this creative, magnetic force *presence* or *listening* or *bearing witness* or any other name, when you are alive in this way, new things can happen. A depth of friendship you haven't known before. An ease and willingness to be yourself, not hiding behind the conventional acceptability you used to worry about. Honesty and kindness, together. Not knowing the answers and not minding how truly open you feel, not minding at all. Present like this, we invite presence in others. It's not something we actually do, of course. It's how we are.

So I suppose you must be wondering what being present has to do with being an elder. Why would having a long life mean that you're conscious, aware, rooted in the present moment? The short answer is, it doesn't mean that. The world is full of old people who seem to lack any jot of awareness. But the longer, truer answer is that presence has quite a lot to do with living a truly mature human life.

Connecting the Dots

I'd like to show you how maturing fits hand in glove with the development of presence. I think this will be clear if we retrace the ripening process we've explored so far.

The first step, as you may recall, was to ask why we're not usually interested in the inner experience of aging. That was when the notion popped up that old age is boring. Seeing this led to the great fog of ideas, beliefs, concepts and plain old lies about what it means to grow old. We saw how most people today have minds thick with these unexamined artifacts from our personal history and Mother Culture's constant humming.

Once you start to notice the chatter in your head, you can pay attention to what it is saying and you don't have to carry it around any longer than you want to. At that point, you've cleared away the biggest obstacle to a conscious presence. Your awareness is no longer enchained; you're free to have moments of openness and clarity.

The second step is what I call cultivation—basically, developing a lively capacity to sense in your inner awareness. Being receptive like this, and in touch with your bodily experience, is what is meant by presence. It's a quality of consciousness where you are rapt, right here and open to the immediacy of the moment.

At this point, we took a third step into what I called 'Opening to the Questions.' This is, in effect, a practice of presence using the inner inquiry process developed by A.H. Almaas. Inquiry is particularly valuable at our stage of life, I believe, because as elders we personally are faced with some of the most profound questions of human existence. Moreover, these are questions that our culture at large dismisses or avoids. So it is no small thing to take up a practice of being present to such questions and to let them guide us, soul-deep, into the truths of our nature.

For the fourth and final step, we turned to the 'hard stuff' that T.S. Eliot named "the gifts reserved for age." If we can have the patience and courage to be present to these experiences, they dissolve our belief in our own immunity, our invulnerability, our separateness. They initiate us into the further mysteries of being human. We become the ones who have descended into the underworld and who can, in time, return to our people bearing gifts of wisdom, compassion, generosity and other essential qualities of mature human beings.

Through all the stages of maturing, however they unfold for each of us, there is a need for presence. You can't mature if you're not present to the experiences that life brings you. Good and bad things happen to everybody. For our experiences to mature us, we can't let them just sit there like so much undigested pizza. We need to be able to digest those experiences: to let them in, feel them, understand them, let them transform in our soul.

Generous

Tonight I opened an email from my friend Harry, the one with the exotic pale blue eyes who told me that aging is not interesting to people like us. Harry had heart surgery last week and he seemed to be recovering beautifully, until suddenly he wasn't. What he wrote—the only thing he wrote—was this: "I'm just realizing that I came within minutes, an hour at most, of dying on Sunday."

I'm just realizing. What happens once we realize how within minutes, an hour at most, we all are? "How close does the dragon's spume have to come," the poet Ellen Bass asks,

How wide does the crack
in heaven have to split?
What would people look like
if we could see them as they are,
soaked in honey, stung and swollen,
reckless, pinned against time?[5]

Once we arrive in the late season of our life, we begin to see people, including ourselves, differently. We know how close the endings are. Not all of us know this, and most of us push the knowing away at least some of the time. But really, we do know and we do see each other and we no longer are fooled, the way we once were, by the surfaces of things.

We no longer believe in the need to thicken our boundaries, shore up our armaments against the enemy at the gates. The gates of our heart are already opening. And what seems to happen then is that the pure presence of ourselves flows as naturally as water into the places that need it. Generous—that's the word we use from an outside perspective. From the inside, it's just natural—a freedom of the heart that won't be held back by the usual polite conventions.

I was reminded of this freedom when I heard a radio interview with Maurice Sendak, the acclaimed illustrator and author of children's books, including most notably, *Where the Wild Things Are*. Sendak was eighty-three at the time and the interviewer, Terry Gross, asked him to talk about his life. "You know," he said, "there is something I'm finding out as I'm aging—that I am in love with the world. … I see my beautiful, beautiful maples that are hundreds and hundreds of years old. And I can *see* how beautiful they are. I can take time to see how beautiful they are. It is a blessing to grow old and have the time."[6]

Sendak went on to explain that his love did not exclude his sorrow. "I cry a lot because I miss people. I cry because they die and I can't stop them. They *leave* me…and I love them more."

At this point I was crying too, at the pure unfettered vulnerability of what this beloved fellow was saying. And then something quite fascinating happened. Terry Gross was moving on, inviting Sendak to talk about his new book which was supposed to be the point of the interview, when he interrupted her. "I want you to know how much you mean to me," he told her. "You have a special gift." And he added, "Almost certainly I'll go before you go." He said that he was glad of that, "so I won't have to miss you."

I could hear the tenderness in his voice, and the interviewer, her professional aplomb teetering for a moment, stuttered softly, "Oh, that's very nice…very nice of you."

Someone said later it was one of the most generous, soul-stirring conversations she'd ever heard on the airwaves. Someone else said that he'd been driving and had to pull his car over to the side of the road because he was weeping. Others told me that they downloaded the interview and played it over for days. Almost always, people used the word *generous* to try to explain what they found so moving.

Generous is the word I thought of too because of the way Sendak held nothing back of himself. It was not simply his words, though they were exquisite, but the full flowing presence of his heart. In that brief hour, in the eight months before Sendak himself was gone, he told us everything important to him, and I think we felt the kindness in that. His pure good-will poured through the airwaves with such grace, wishing us all good things, urging us, "Live your life, live your life, live your life!"

Being Vulnerable

Most of what I've written so far is based on what demographers call the Young-Old stage of life. Falling in the range between fifty-five to seventy-five years, it has also been called the Third Age, Adulthood II and the Age of Active Wisdom. Basically, all of those names serve to distinguish this time from *Later*—the Old-Old, the 'frail elderly.'[7]

I have focused on the earlier stage because it is the one I know so far. But I don't want to catapult over the vulnerability and dependency that is likely to come if we live long enough to grow very old. Because, like death, we can't leave this out. To know that *we* are vulnerable—and not just *them*, the ones who are five or ten or twenty years older—is more uncomfortable than death for some of us. I talked to a woman in her seventies who regularly volunteers at a senior center, with people in various stages of dementia.

"I keep all that separate from me," she confided.

"I understand," I said, because unfortunately I do. Separating *us* from *them* is so familiar to me. It's what I was trying to escape when I left my cushy job at the University of Toronto to work on the geriatric wards at Sunnybrook Hospital. I wanted to get past the separation of doctors/patients, researchers/subjects that made me feel so lonely. But now at the edge of my consciousness, I can spot my inner age accountant tallying up all the ways I'm not really *that* old yet. So here I am again, caught in the separation, so secretly contented to be a Young-Old rather than an Old-Old as if it were something permanent and real, as if it were a secure nest I could remain in for the length of my days.

Even with so few years' difference; even when we know, rationally, how close the ending is; even now, it so appealing to believe in ourselves as the giver, the helper, the benevolent one and to make a nice distance from being the one who needs help. We like to be counted in, as a player, not sent to sit out the game on the sidelines. It's so normal to want this in our culture. Whole swaths of our political process are shaped to the need to be independent of Big Government (but don't touch my Social Security payments!) And of course, generosity too can be distorted in the service of this need.

William Thomas, the founder of the Greenhouse Movement for alternatives to nursing homes, is very good at skewering this Young-Old tendency to distance ourselves from our vulnerability. He's extraordinary in his compassion for the oldest old people and razor-wire sharp in his description of the Young-Old whom he calls the "kings and queens of volunteerism." He says that people at this earlier stage are afraid of losing their status as adults, so they volunteer to build houses, deliver meals, and organize voter registration drives. But hidden in the "can-do ideology" is anxiety. It's easy to spot the anxiety, he says. Just look for a single telltale word: *still*. The volunteers are "still active, still contributing, still a valuable member of the community of adults, still faithful to doing, getting, and having."[8]

I wasn't kidding about the razor wire, was I? But I have to admit, he does have a point. Several points. The main one is that it is a delusion—at whatever stage of life—to believe that there is any wisdom or truth to denying our vulnerability; to pretending that we are not profoundly, touchingly, irrevocably interdependent on each other for our well-being and our lives.

I know this theoretically, but even writing it down makes me uneasy. The vulnerability of advanced old age is what I was hoping to avoid when I tried to give away Mary Morrison's question about *diminishment* to my elders' group in Berkeley. It is, as one of the women acknowledged, the stinky stuff under the carpet that nobody wants to talk about. I know a lot about growing very old and I can talk about it, but am I willing to feel it? Not yet, Lord. I still have five more years, demographically. Or maybe more if I go to yoga more often and lift weights for my skinny arms and a bunch of other things that I actually can't remember right now.

So I guess it's obvious where my inquiry needs to go: being present to the vulnerability of the last life-stage. That, after all, is ripening too. It's the culmination of the process. Can I be conscious all the way through my life to the very end? I want to be. I don't want to miss any part of this life.

Except for the frailty. Maybe I can get an exemption on that one.

A Necessary Part of the Whole

In spite of my wish for an exemption, I know that it doesn't work to make exiles of our experiences. Being present as an elder means including everything: dependency and our fear of it; generosity and wisdom and whatever qualities are developing now; the fragility of our skin; the way the walls we've built around us are dissolving; and the way they're not dissolving at all but hanging on for dear life. It means including all of what we feel and know and fear and love as a necessary part of our humanness, a necessary part of the whole. Nothing left out and, when possible, no love held back.

Because, to exaggerate wildly to express how I feel, elders are the ones in charge of celebrations. We're the ones in charge of knowing that everyone and everything fits, that there can be no exiles in our undivided humanness. And we are the ones to affirm our kinship across time and space, so that the people of our time can bridge the true continuity of all those who have gone before us with all who will come after us—all of them our relatives, all of them our ancestors, all of them our grandchildren.

Chapter 12

Ancestors

I am part of a network of events
that have occurred in the lives of many people,
some of whom are unknown to me.
…. To be aware of this is to carry their love within my heart,
and to live in a spirit of gratitude.
~Roxanne Lanier, *The Communion of Saints*[1]

Invitations come our way as we age. Some come from younger friends asking for maps, and others come from our own elders, as they leave absences for us to fill. Still others we rarely notice until we have become elders ourselves. These are from the ancestors.

In ages before our own, elders were understood to be bridges between the world of everyday and the world to come. Without elders to link to the ancestors, it was believed that the people would be orphans, cut off from their guiding stories, traditions, meanings, history, arts, and most of all, from the continuity of life beyond death.

Like most of our modern Western world, I hadn't given a lot of thought to ancestors. When I did, I mostly remembered the black altars in homes I'd visited in Japan and Korea, where tiny bits of food, alcohol, and sometimes cigarettes were laid out regularly for deceased relatives. For a long time, I dismissed ancestors as something that had meaning for people in cultures and times far from my own.

But I see things differently now. I include all those who have gone before me as my relatives and my tribe, as kin. This almost always seems to begin in lands where I think I am a stranger. It has happened in Holland and Poland and in Germany, and most recently, in Croatia where I learned to know myself as an elder connected to those generations who have gone before me and to the children yet to come.

The Necessity of Grieving

An October morning in Dubrovnik, 2010. Clouds have been layering over the perfect blue horizon since sunrise—feathers drifting toward Italy in the west, splatters of white floating north to Slovenia, and tiny cream puffs piling up like crockenbouches in the south over Bosnia. Sitting here with two pillows plumped behind my back, I am living one of my childhood dreams, lazing in bed and gazing out at the endless sky.

"Another day in Paradise," Paul announces, coming in to tickle my feet so I'll get out of bed and join him for tea. He's looking crisp in his khakis and sports jacket, and he's already finished breakfast. I pad into the living room in my pajamas as he's packing up his computer for a quick stroll to a branch of the University of Zagreb. He's here for a conference on climate change sponsored by the Norwegian government and an assortment of other governmental agencies, including the European Union. I'm here as the spouse.

"What are you doing today?"

"No idea," I wave airily. "Maybe the beach?"

It's great. I've always wanted to be The Spouse (for short shifts). Marvelous open spaces of no plans, cloud gazing, not knowing where I'll walk, or if I'll even bother to leave our little balcony for the town below. Time out of time. Whereabouts unknown. In the cool of the evening, I dress up and make my way down the 350 stone steps leading to the sea. There's an esplanade along the water that leads into the massive Pile Gate. From there it's an easy walk to meet Paul and his colleagues, academics and media people from across Europe and Africa, at one of the open air restaurants along the water.

But you know how sometimes what is so good at one level, so

shining and bright, can have a cold, dark current running at another level? I'm feeling that now. It's about a war that officially ended in 1995. Paul and I were here seven years after that war when Dubrovnik's walls were still pock-marked with shrapnel from their Serbian neighbors in the course of the six constituent republics of Yugoslavia tearing themselves apart. We had travelled to Croatia for a peace conference when the peace was still shaky. And later, as we drove north through the small towns of the Dalmatian Coast into Slovenia, we were shaky too, off balance. On the surface, we saw freshly-painted houses and repaired roads. But—how to say this?—we felt blood from the killings pooled on the streets. Our eyes saw bright new beginnings, but something inside us was shredding apart. We drove with our friend Bernard, a Belgian finance expert not known for his emotionality, but we all felt this underlying, disorienting grief.

Now, fifteen years later, travel agencies offer special bus trips to Mostar, Montenegro, Ljublijana. In the advertisements, buildings that exploded on the TV news in the nineties stand intact, as if nothing had ever happened. Once again, young men leap into the Neretva River from the stone walls of the exquisite Stari Most, the bridge built by Suleiman the Magnificent and intentionally destroyed by the Bosnian Croats.

The people have moved on, I tell myself. Get over it. Leathery-skinned old women in bikinis gossip on the beach, young couples neck under the awnings, and old men smoke and shout at each other over miniscule cups of cappuccino at the roadside cafes. The cars are relatively new, and the shelves of the local markets are well stocked.

I try to figure this out: why I am having such a hard time letting go of the past when all around me the Croatians are going on with their lives?

It's because I'm a tourist, I think, just passing through. I haven't caught up because I haven't grieved the losses that were suffered here.

I didn't know I needed to.

How do you know what you have to grieve? Surely you can't grieve every war that shows up on the news, I tell myself. A cruise-ship's horn startles me with a loud, mournful blast. Again and again the horn blares, long and heavy. Grieving is grieving, it seems to say. Who are you to decide what you should and should not mourn? The soul feels what it feels. If you turn away from that, you turn away from your humanity.

Where did I get the idea that I shouldn't mourn? Or only mourn for certain people and not others? As I follow my questions, I understand that some ideas come from my family, but not only from them. Our modern culture says that grieving is something to get through as soon as possible; that it serves no good purpose to feel the ache of losses and grieve for the ways we suffer and cause suffering. The best medicine, we learn, is to cheer up and move on, as if grieving and moving on were mutually exclusive.

Yesterday I got a strong dose of this medicine.

Sinagoga

I'd found my way in the Old City to *Zudioska ulica*, Jew's Street, on one of the alleyways leading off the *Stradun*, the main promenade. Getting directions in a pizza shop, I arrived at #5, an old house with a sign announcing *Sinagoga*, 15 kuna. Mounting the steep stairs to the second floor, I gave my *kuna* to a bored-looking young man who handed me a ticket.

"What time are Shabbat services this week?" I asked brightly, thinking I'd like to sing prayers in Hebrew with Croatians.

"No services," he said.

"No services?"

"Only on High Holidays."

I wanted to make some contact with him. (Hey, hello. Are you Jewish? What's it like living here? I'm Jewish too. I grew up in

New Jersey.)

I figured that was way too over-friendly American and tried for something more neutral.

"How large is the Jewish community?"

"Forty-five."

"So no rabbi?"

"No rabbi," he replied in the same flat voice. And finally, to get rid of me, "Go up to the synagogue first, then come down to the museum on this floor."

Everything is so smooth in Dubrovnik, worn with age like the medieval paving stones on the promenade and the satin banisters in the churches. The wooden stairs going up to the third-story synagogue are smooth, and so is the railing I hold as I climb the final stairs to the women's section at the very top of the house. Looking down, I can see the central bimah, elevated, with hanging brass oil lamps above it. Around the sides, high dark wooden seats are built into the walls. The guidebook tells me that in 1652 this house was turned into a synagogue, about a hundred years after the Dubrovnik Republic "allowed Jews to settle within the city ramparts."

I sit for a while in the women's section and then descend to the main floor, wandering around and touching the cool dark wood. I wonder what to do in this sad, empty shell of a synagogue with no people who worship here. Where did everybody go? And how come the city of Dubrovnik has made such a big deal of preserving this house? A red-headed woman with tortoiseshell eyeglasses interrupts my musings with her flash camera, ignoring a sign with a slash line across a camera. I head downstairs to the museum.

Two very old Torahs lie open in a glass cabinet. A sign says that they date from the thirteenth to the seventeenth centuries and "bear witness to Dubrovnik's Jewish community throughout six centuries of history." I'm a bit shocked to see these venerable Torahs displayed as if they were commodities and not portals to a living faith. (I get just as upset at anthropology museums that fill their cabinets with ceremonial feather-fans and sacred medicine-pipes.)

I want to take whoever immured these Torahs and shake them till their teeth rattle. Instead, I sigh and move on to the next exhibit. Suddenly what has happened here breaks in on me. I'm looking at a yellow armband with a black star of David printed on it. The next exhibit is the order for confiscation of Jewish books, and after that the order for confiscation of Jewish property, and then the deportation order for all Jews from the city of Dubrovnik. I'm crying by the time I get to a list of names with a scroll drawn around them. Two vines with thorns curl down the scroll, and at the bottom, under the dates 1941-1944, a small sign reads, 'Died in the Holocaust.' Now the red-haired lady with the camera has come in and is hugging me. Telling me it is okay and there is no point in crying and I should stop.

"Look," she says, "I see it this way. The synagogue is still here. We're still here. You have to let the past go."

She leaves but I can't seem to stop crying. There is no place to sit down so I put on my sunglasses and go out past the kid who is taking tickets.

"Take care," he says, not in a monotone. I go outside and sit on the stone steps. I'm still crying when a tall fellow with a plummy British accent comes over and tells me we must move on.

"You have to let it go," he says. Not unkindly. Just sure that what he is telling me is something I need to hear. Then he pats me on the shoulder and walks away.

I keep crying on the stone steps outside the second oldest synagogue in Europe for as long as I need to, a good long time. Not only for my people but for the Croatian people and the Serbs and the Bosnians, for the Muslim women who were raped in the concentration camps and for the men who raped them, and for the children who will carry the marks of these wars and most likely pass them on to their children. I'm crying for all of us and the wars we make on each other because as Biff says in *Death of a Salesman*, "Attention must be paid." And as he doesn't say but I would add, because we must grieve whatever comes to us as a sorrow. We have to let our tears flow so that we don't lose touch with our raw and beautiful hearts, with the core of what it means to be human. And while I believe that this need exists for all people, it seems to me to be particularly the place of elders to bear witness. And to grieve when grief is called for.

Calling the Names

About a month later, after a few weeks of teaching a seminar in Holland, I'm on my way back to California. Settling into my window seat for the short flight from Amsterdam to Frankfurt, I end up deep in conversation with a man in horn-rimmed glasses sitting next to me. I'd intended to hide behind the pages of the *Herald Tribune* but couldn't resist his open, almost eager face. He's Greek, he says, a music professor fresh from teaching in Brooklyn, on his way to Frankfurt to learn how to conduct an orchestra. He tells me his name, Nichos something, and asks for mine. Sherry, I say.

"What about your last name," he asks. "I am very interested in names. I make a kind of study of them."

I tell him that my last name doesn't mean anything to me. My parents changed our name when I was twelve. I think they wanted something that sounded more American.

"Same with me," he says, "no link either. My father changed our name when he lived in Austria so he would fit in better, wouldn't sound so Greek."

In the way of strangers who tell each other intimate things, I find myself talking to Nichos about the list of names I saw in Dubrovnik. "I was wandering through an old synagogue," I tell him, "wondering where everyone had gone. Then I walked downstairs and found the display and the scroll with names."

I don't tell him how I couldn't stop crying. But because he leans forward to hear my words over the plane's muffled roar and his eyes are kind, I say that I wanted to read the names out loud, to recite them like a prayer or a blessing. I don't mention that last part about the prayer either. I'm trying to monitor the intimacy a little, not just blurt out my whole inner process to a guy I don't even know.

"Names are important," he says. "Sometimes I go to old cemeteries when I'm in Greece to recite the names carved into the headstones."

I like to go to cemeteries, too. I've been doing it since my thirties. And if the cemetery is Jewish and no one is around, I chant prayers for the ancestors, like Nichos reciting the names. It just feels companionable, but not something I've ever thought about or want to discuss with a stranger at 35,000 feet. There seems to be nothing left to say so I turn to gaze out at the vast fields of clouds.

About a half hour later, Nichos says, "Sometimes names have to be hidden."

He says this casually, breaking the silence as if we'd been talking all the while. And then he tells me a story that he heard from his mother when he was a small boy in Delphi. The story is about the island of Zakynthos at the time of the Nazi occupation in 1943.

"Almost as soon as the army marched onto the island," he told me, "the commander demanded a list of all the Jews living on the island."

"That's what happened in Dubrovnik, too," I say.

"Yes, but in this case the mayor said he'd need several days to put a list together. In the meantime, he and the bishop sent word to the people of the island and within days, all 275 Jews were safely hidden in the mountain villages. And every one of them survived the occupation."

"But what about the Nazi commandant? He must have

insisted on getting that list of names."

"Oh yes. The mayor and the bishop got together on that. They handed the list over to the commandant a week later. It had only two names on it—Mayor Lucas Karrer and Bishop Chrysostomos."

* * *

It's been about a month now and Nichos' story, together with the list of names I saw in the Dubrovnik synagogue, seem to have formed themselves into question that won't go away. I'm not sure what the question is—it doesn't have words yet. But there is something haunting about Nichos reciting the names on Greek headstones, and his story about Zakynthos, and my wanting to chant the names on the scroll as if they were words in a prayer. There seems to be something that I keep passing over.

I have what might be a clue. It's a photograph I took on the day I left Dubrovnik. I'd made a hasty last minute trip to the Old City to have another look at the scroll with the names of the dead. When I'd climbed the steps of the synagogue and reached the room with the scroll, I felt an almost irresistible impulse to pull it off the wall, bundle it in velvet wrappings and run down the stairs cradling it to me as if it were a sacred Torah and I were its rescuer. Fortunately, some shred of sanity prevailed and I rummaged through my backpack for my cell phone and snapped a (forbidden) photo. Then, shaken, I hurried into the Adriatic sunshine to pick up Paul and catch a cab to the airport.

Once I got back to California, I kept bringing up the photo on my computer screen to stare at it, as if it held the answer to the question I didn't know how to ask. After a week of doing this, I started to wonder about the Hebrew writing on either side of the list of names. The names were written in the standard alphabet but what was the Hebrew? Torah passages? I emailed my nephew who is a rabbi in Los Angeles and attached the photo of the scroll.

"The Hebrew is just the names you read in the standard alphabet. They have been rewritten in Hebrew and placed as if they were in a Torah to give them more sanctity," he wrote back. "Hope that is helpful."

I blew up the photo and looked at it more closely. And then slowly, without thinking about it, I began sounding the Hebrew letters one by one, the names stumbling out with my halting pronunciation, the way I read prayers as a child. I never learned to read smoothly without the vowel markings, so as I read the names from the Hebrew letters, I had to go back and forth to the standard alphabet to get them right. I did this stubbornly, wanting to feel the names in my mouth taking their form out of the Hebrew letters: Salamon Baruch. Mosi Tolentino. Rafael Tolentino. Josef Berner. As I called the names of the ones who were taken away, they set off depth charges inside me, like soundings from beyond time.

Names as prayers. Names as blessings. Saying the names was the answer to the question I hadn't known how to ask. In the Zen Center where I once lived, the great iron bell sounded each morning as we called the names of our teacher and his teacher, tracing our connection through a lineage of awakened masters back to the Buddha. Sonja Margulies, a Zen teacher, recites the names of the women who have guided and loved her, beginning with her own mother and grandmothers, and continuing on in a great circle of interconnection to her aunties and friends and her own teachers throughout her lifetime. Joanna Macy, the Buddhist activist, calls the names of her lineage like this: Horned Owl, Grey Wolf, Seal, Raccoon, Tiger, Great Sequoia. She does this not only as an affirmation of the web of life, she says, but so she can bear to feel her grief and her love for the ones who have disappeared from the Earth. So she can find the courage to speak out for the sake of the children to come.

As I near 70, I, too, take my place as an elder, a lineage carrier, for those who have gone before me and those who will come after me. I begin by calling the names on the Dubrovnik scroll, then Mayor Lucas Karrer and Bishop Chrysostomos, then I remember the ones without names, the 275 Jews they kept hidden. I honor the memory of my father and Nichos' father and all those who thought they had to change their names to fit in, and all of our grandmothers' grandmothers whose full names have been forgotten. I want the sounds of those names not just to resonate but to reverberate so that they do not end abruptly. I want them to reach beyond time to the unlimited, the unbounded, ringing through the world we have now into the world to come, to the infinite silence within all names and sounds. I take my place as an elder by calling the names and hearing their reverberations, by honoring those who have gone before us and blessing the children of the future. May we all take our place as elders when we are ready to do so. May we become links, witnesses, bridges for our human community to the continuity of life beyond the boundaries of birth and death.

PART V

HARVEST

What comes next?

Once the ripening wheat ripples through the fields and the corn is high, the next chapter is something we all know, isn't it? For 10,000 years, the survival of our species has depended on the harvest. You clear the land, you plant and cultivate your crops, and God willing, you reap the good harvest for your people. The 'God willing' part is not incidental. No one with actual experience of the harvest takes it for granted. In North America we have our favorite holiday of Thanksgiving. Around the world from ancient times to today, we create rituals and festivals to give thanks to Mother Earth, to God, to Allah, to the great goddesses of the grain and the corn and the gods of the vineyards and the wine. Thanks that we'll have what we need to make it through the long winter, the dry season, the fallow time. Thanks that we've been able to bring in, finally, the abundance. Thanks that our children will eat well and thrive.

And what about us? What about the elders who more than ever before in history are ripening into maturity? Will there be the equivalent of a good harvest? A cause for thanksgiving?

In the next few decades, about two billion people over sixty are expected on the planet. One in every four of us will be an elder. Imagine what it would be like if even a fair-sized proportion of these elders develop wisdom, generosity, long-sighted vision and the kind of love that extends not only to their own children and grandchildren but to all children.

It would change our world.

Elders who can hear the cries of the world can tell it like it is. Aware of their own death, mature elders can feel free from the need to succeed or impress or curry favor with anyone. Imagine that—mature human beings who are not afraid to speak the truth of what they see and stand for what they value! Then imagine that people like this, in immense numbers, create circles of peers to contemplate the urgent needs of our time; that they join with people of all ages to transform how we communicate with each other, what we invest in and what kind of future we commit to building. The global climate crisis and all that unravels in its wake, the nuclear threat, violence in our schools and public places, violence against women worldwide, lack of choices for young people in developing countries—the need for wise and compassionate decisions could not be more searingly obvious.

The key question, I think, is about the transition. How do we get to the harvest from here? We have the essentials: an evolutionary jump in elders who can become mature and a need for mature wisdom that grows more urgent by the day. But the harvest is never a given. It takes immense co-operation and planning and hard work and a lot of things I didn't know anything about when I started writing the next chapter.

At this point, developing maturity has been largely an individual process. It's personal, something that that takes place out of sight of the public eye. But the scale of what is happening now is, as you know, vast and teeming with diversity. For our new longevity to be fruitful, it will need cultivation, support, inspiration, and welcoming. I invite you to consider with me what we'll need to reap the abundance of this ripening time. To start with, I thought I'd better find out what it really means to bring in the harvest.

Chapter 13

Lessons From the Harvest

As I settled down to think about our transition from a time of individual ripening selves to millions of elders maturing, I knew that I'd better phone my friend Marcia. She grew up in the cornfields of the Midwest and I, as you may recall, come from Atlantic City. I consider myself an expert on sand (in carpets, socks and bathing suits), how to flirt with life guards (in 1959) and the best way to dive into a breaking wave. But a harvest? Marcia was laughing before I even finished explaining my problem. "Yeah, okay," she said, "I'll tell you about harvesting corn in Iowa. But it wasn't easy, you know." I suppose she issued this warning in case I was harboring any gauzy East Coast fantasies about hayrides and big orange moons. (I was.)

In the years before she left home for college, Marcia's father broke with tradition and taught his daughters to drive the tractors and the balers and the trucks, to stack hay bales and load corn from the fields into wagons. "My dad wasn't particularly easy to harvest with," she said, but even after many difficult seasons, images of abundance remain: "the wagons so full they're rocking down the road to the elevators, and the combines with corn shiny as gold coins glistening down the chutes. It's all with me still, and so is the sense of completion when the fields were clean and we could rest."

I was starting to get the overwhelming sense of harvest plenty that can fill you day after day after day and I tried to picture millions of human beings actually growing into fullness like that. But before I got too dreamy, Marcia insisted that I understand two other things: the harvest happens in a tight window of time and it takes everybody working hard and working together to bring it off.

"You've got to get the crops in before the snow falls or they'll spoil, so there's this urgency and you're working achingly long days. But it's fun, too, because you're all together—the neighbors from the other farms, the hired guys from town, and your own family. Harvest is such a peak time, you see. There's such a vitality, such a sense of goodness when everything comes together like that."

Imagine the 21st century as a peak time for human maturity—a time when the urgent need for our species to grow up is balanced by a long enough lifespan in which to do it. If you try to picture this, you'll likely stumble into something familiar: our culture's sticky presumptions about growing old. These explicit opinions and unconscious certainties make us think that we know all about what it means to age when in fact we know very little. And even worse, they kill our curiosity about what the new longevity means for us personally and for our world. As a result, something sad and, to my mind, utterly unnecessary happens. We decide that old age is boring while all around us, its fruits are ripening into sumptuous flavors.

I heard a story recently from a vineyard owner named Jacques that reminds me of our cultural delusion about aging. In the last century, he said, mature vineyards were regarded as treasures because their grapes produced a deliciously wide spectrum of flavors. But now such vineyards and orchards are routinely ploughed under after twenty years.

"Why plough them under?" I asked, horrified.

"Because the Internal Revenue Service offers depreciations for only that long. As a result, we have wines that are very fruity and nice, but they're not complex. Not rich. The vines with the fullest flavors have been lost."

He concluded wryly, "So today, a vineyard, an orchard, is in a category with office machines. What you can't depreciate anymore, you get rid of." His cynicism, I supposed, covered his grief.

Lessons from the Harvest

I decided I needed to hear more of what Jacques could tell me about the grape harvest. The meeting was partly Marcia's idea. She worried that her experiences in the Iowa cornfields were not enough to help me understand harvests. "There you are, right next to the wine country," she said. "Call somebody who has a vineyard and invite him to tea."

So on a bright December afternoon, Jacques was sipping green tea in my living room and I was sitting across from him, nibbling on the camembert I'd bought for the occasion.

"Harvest." Jacques pronounced the word slowly, as if he was sampling a glass of wine and considering its possibilities. He didn't start with the harvest, however, even though I asked him about it right away. He took his time, describing first how his grandparents moved the family home from Alsace to Paris but he returned in the summers to work in his cousins' vineyards; how he came to California in his twenties and learned about wine from a neighbor; and then, in his forties, he bought a vineyard in Sonoma at the end of a narrow road. He called his winery Dry Creek. It was set in a bowl of steeply rising hills, a perfect location, he said, for the wines he wanted to produce, the kind that come from a particular place and tell you about their origins.

Then, finally, we were ready to talk about the harvest. "I guess the most basic thing I can say is that it's not just the act of taking fruit from the vine." He spoke softly with a slight French accent so I had to lean forward to hear. "It's the whole process," he explained. "Selecting the site, choosing the line of grapes to plant, planting and training the vines and then all the cyclical practices you do all through the growing time."

I tried to imagine what cyclical practices meant. He must have noticed me struggling because he named them: pruning, ploughing if you're on a hillside; cultivating; deciding whether or not to irrigate; additives you work into the ground and deciding whether they'll be natural or not. And so forth.

"Picking the fruit is just *one* act in the whole process," he repeated, emphasizing the *one*.

By this time I realized that I was being guided by an expert into the secrets of the "crush," as harvests are called in the wine country. I was fascinated. Paul and I had lived in Sonoma for several years but had never found our way into the inner world of the vineyards. So I dropped whatever agenda I had and moved closer to Jacques so I could hear better and learn about the lessons of the harvest.

1. Pay attention to the whole process.

This was Jacques' first point, as he carefully laid out his own origins as a winemaker and then proceeded to trace the development of the harvest from choosing a vineyard location to making wine.

I wondered what it would be like to live in a culture that took whole-process learning seriously, one where you were supported and inspired to develop consciously through your entire life cycle. In the days that followed, I dreamed of creating places and occasions where people of all ages could spin and weave the fabric for this way of life. Right from the beginning, we'd be naming and shaking free from Mother Culture's sticky "appropriate age" projections on each other: the sexy ingénue, the depressed dude going through his mid-life crisis, the pompous old guy who thinks he knows everything, the crone who has nothing to say, the kids who fuss with their hairdos and nose rings. I thought about how we'd need to invent and invest in stories, theatre, films and music to fire up our collective imagination. And how we'd design social networks and blogs and international teleconferences and whatever innovations we'd need to let us come together anywhere and everywhere to create what we needed.

2. Work together. Nobody brings in the harvest alone.

Like Marcia's stories from the Iowa cornfields, Jacques had Sonoma tales of cousins and sisters and brother-in-laws and uncles of his full-time crew arriving for the crush in a spirit of "enormous camaraderie and good will." Retired now, Jacques was a bit wistful recalling "the extraordinary sense of all of us working together."

I couldn't help worrying about the age-segregation in our society. We'll have to find ways around or through the walls that keep us apart because we absolutely need cross-fertilization. I wondered how we'd do this. After all, working with a great diversity of age and experience isn't easy. But then I remembered how the elders in Portland, Maine listened to all the conflicting sides in their community—really listened—and how that made even the most opinionated adversaries begin to listen to each other. I thought, too, of how the poet Sandy Scull doubted that he had anything of value to say to young vets returning from Iraq and Afghanistan. It turned out that what Sandy lived through as a marine in Vietnam and what he worked through in the forty years afterwards had great value indeed.

When you travel through the dark places of wisdom over decades, you can return bearing gifts. I've learned that from the elders I've worked with in circles and seminars from Alaska to Amsterdam, Toronto to Mobile. When you wrestle with the angels of loss and endings that aging inevitably brings, you develop a skill for listening and sometimes for giving words to the unsayable. The quality of presence you bring can sometimes dissolve boundaries and create trust beyond anything the ordinary mind can account for. When elders work together and when they join in wider alliances, extraordinary things can happen.

3. Find the balance between the urgent need of the time and readiness of your grapes, and expect the unexpected.

The harvest is a crucible. In the cornfields, you hurry to avoid the snow; in the vineyards, it's the rain. "If you're late and it rains," Jacques told me, "the clusters begin to rot from the inside out. But you can't be too early because you need to catch the peak of ripeness. So there's an urgency to find the just-in-time balance." He said that sometimes white grapes ripen before the reds and the harvest extends over weeks. But at other times, the grapes ripen all at once and you all have to work around the clock.

"What does that mean?"

"Three in the morning till ten at night."

Oh.

"We always prepared for the harvest as if it were predictable," he said, "and it never was." Repairing the pumps and presses and cleaning and oiling all the equipment, putting fresh paint on the boxes where the grapes are stored...but you never knew for sure.

For elders, the urgency is personal. The years we have left are limited. But the need for haste is planetary as well, pulling us all in. As I write this, Australia is burning in huge swaths across New South Wales. One prominent researcher commented: "Those of us who spend our days trawling—and contributing to—the scientific literature on climate change are becoming increasingly gloomy about the future of human civilization."[1] Scientists are long past the time of niceties, she said, "of avoiding the dire nature of what is unfolding, and politely trying not to scare the public."

Can the facts be any more raw? It is long past time for us to know what's happening and yet there is an absence of what almost everyone seems content to call "political will." There is a great need for politicians to take action on climate change, for voters to insist on it and for the mainstream media to report the truth of what is happening. The objective need of our time is devastatingly clear. We need to do all we can to develop the courage, wisdom and the will to speak up and stand for our shared future.

One example of an exemplary elder voice has come from Retired General Stanley McChrystal. Speaking in January of 2013, in the wake of a series of devastating shootings in schools and movie theaters and shopping centers across the United States, he said that he had spent his military service carrying the kinds of guns now allowed in the public places. "I personally don't think there's any need for that kind of weaponry on the streets and particularly around the schools in America," he said. "I understand everybody's desire to have whatever they want—but we have to protect our children and our police and we have to protect our population. I think we have to take a very mature look at that."[2]

4. In the final analysis, the transformation is a miracle.

As Jacques and I were coming to the end of our conversation, he thought of one more thing he wanted to tell me. "Remember, our purpose in picking grapes is to make wine. In the final analysis, after all the effort to plant and cultivate and pick the grapes, the fermentation of grapes into wine is an absolute miracle. Of course, we help the process along but the transformation would happen if we did nothing. I can't think of an organic product that won't change itself if you give it enough time."

That's how it is with human beings, too, wouldn't you say? Maturing is not exactly something we *do*. It's a process of change we engage, a softening of the heart, a relaxing of the shell we once thought we needed to be safe; it's saying "Yes" to life even before you know the question. As I look back on my own life, it seems to me that maturing is hard work—and ultimately, a miracle.

* * *

Jacques stood to put on his coat. "You know, in wine country the crush is a very big deal and everyone's always asking 'How's the crush going? How's the crush?' But most people don't have the patience to listen. So I never talk about how it's really going. I just smile and say, 'Fine. It's going fine.'"

I don't want to do that here. It's not all fine, not really. Our culture, our whole planet, is in desperate need of wise, compassionate, courageous people of real maturity. Maybe we would get to that point given enough time, as Jacques believes, but the truth is that we don't have time. We need to grow up as human beings as soon as possible. We need to grow up yesterday.

We have multitudes of elders maturing now. To bring what is ripening to a good harvest, we'll need to work together. We'll need a steadfast, persistent willingness—not only 'political will'—and passion and long-term vision and unfettered creativity and other resources so new they're still gestating in the field of the possible. And one more thing: we'll need to change the future of aging.

Creating the Future

At the end of World War II, a Dutch Jew who had survived the war in hiding published a survey called, in its English translation, *The Image of the Future*.[3] Fred Polak studied 1500 years of history to understand how a culture's vision of what the future can be shapes the life it actually lives. With a positive image of the future, people invested in education, in schools and roads and bridges and communication lines, in all varieties of new businesses and institutions. Even if they turned out to be mistaken in the details of what they imagined, the results were still quite positive. And if a culture lacked a positive vision of the future, Polak showed, its creative power withered and the culture itself stagnated. Negative images were even more destructive, leading to hopelessness and helplessness. The collective pessimism seeped into everything, resulting in people snatching and grabbing to secure whatever they could for themselves and their families.

Our future is something that we participate in creating.

Isn't that an amazing statement? It makes me have to sit back and scratch my head and just let it percolate for awhile. This is what Polak asserted, and his assertion helped to launch an entire discipline of scenario building and future studies. The work that Paul Ray and I present in *The Cultural Creatives* and that Paul reports in *The Emerging Planetary Wisdom Culture* describes some of the recent research that supports Polak's conclusion. Quite reliably, people who live from positive guiding images are willing to act (and vote) for the sake of a better world.[4] We are a future-creating species. There are great consequences to how we focus our collective imagination.

When it comes to aging, our collective imagination has been focused on pessimism. If we stay trapped in those dismal images of growing old—or, equally bad, in the infomercial versions of golden agers golfing into the sunset—the genuine gifts of conscious aging will wither on the vine. As Fred Polak might have put it, what we envision about aging will shape our future.

But we can change our minds. As a culture, we can set our intention to question our expectations about aging and challenge them in ourselves and in each other with great zest and insistence and imagination. Maybe we'll be fierce. Or funny. Or outrageous. Maybe a billion elders and all their friends will emerge as flash mobs in town plazas, making music and dancing and then creating spaces for dialogues and deep conversation. What we envision can invite new guiding scenarios for our planet and new forms of communities for elders, including co-housing and green houses and artists' collectives.

Oh yes, we can each set our intention to do whatever we're inspired to contribute. We can call two friends who call two friends and start a circle of elders. And we'll need to create other circles that are big enough and wide enough to seed a basis for real change. We'll want to include people of all ages because nobody brings in the harvest alone. Not elders. Not women. Not Americans or Europeans or Asians or Australians, or Africans.

The urgency of our time and the unprecedented billions of elders on the planet make a fertile field for a fundamental mind change about our future. As in the harvest, everyone who wants to be included is needed now. To do whatever you can do: expose a lie about growing old; delve into the mysteries and subtleties of aging; reap the generosity and kindness and wisdom that come from being present through losses and endings; and in any and all the ways you can find, deepen your humanity through the breadth and length of your years.

After All, the Harvest

After all, we are each so unique. The gifts we're given, the circumstances we're born into, all that we develop and collide with along the way—who can say what the harvest of each life will be? And who can claim that each lifetime has only a single harvest, and not seasons of ripening and seasons of lying fallow, each growing out of and enriching the one that follows?

Maturity is not what you act like, or look like; not how photo-genic you are with your white hair and wrinkles or how many stories you may or may not be able to tell. And I think it is not even an openness of mind, a perspective that takes in the long-term view, though that is a great gift.

Maturity, it seems to me, is what has been gestating and growing in you all these years, a wholehearted humanness. And I believe it is a willingness to stand by, to stand for, what you love. To reach the true harvest of our lives, the point is not to know the map but to be the map. The point is to mature not for ourselves alone but for all our kin, all those who have gone before us and the children of the future.

End Notes

CHAPTER 1. WHEN YOUR MIND IS NOT CLOUDED

1. Laura L. Carstensen, director of the Stanford Center for Longevity, in her book *A Long Bright Future*. New York: Broadway Books, 2009. p 3.
2. Excerpt from *"The Lobster Quadrille,"* Lewis Carroll's *Alice's Adventures in Wonderland*. London:1865. (original publication.)

PART II

1. R.F.C. Hull, trans. "The Stages of Life," in *The Portable Jung*, ed. Joseph Campbell (New York: Viking, 1971), 16-17. Cited in Nicholas Delbanco's *Lastingness: The Art of Old Age*. (my spacing)

CHAPTER 3. WE ARE ALREADY NAKED

1. Excerpt from Ellen Bass "If You Knew," *The Human Line*. Copper Canyon Press, 2007.
2. W.S. Merwin, "Worn Words."

CHAPTER 4. WHEN YOUR MIND IS NOT CLOUDED

1. Zen Master Wu-Men Kui-k'ai (1183-1260) is the author of the famous koan text, The Gateless Gate (Wu Man Kuan).
2. *www.harposplace.com*

CHAPTER 5. ESCAPING MOTHER CULTURE'S WEB

1. Gertrude Stein, *Geographical History of America*. New York: Vintage, 1973. P 63.
2. Daniel Quinn, *Ishmael*. New York: Bantam, 1995. Pp36-7.
3. Jim Thomas directed me to this clear account in Alistair MacIntyre's *Dependent Rational Animal*. Chicago: Open Court, 1999. P. 2.

"And when the ill, the injured and the otherwise disabled are presented in the pages of moral philosophy books, it is almost always exclusively as possible subjects of benevolence by moral agents who are themselves presented as though they are continuously rational, healthy and untroubled. So we are invited, when we do think of disability, to think of "the disabled" as "them," as other than "us," as a separate class, not as ourselves as we have been, sometimes are now and may be in the future."

4. Mary Catherine Bateson 's term, from *Composing a Future Life*. New York: Alfred A. Knopf, 2010.

CHAPTER 6. SECRETS & SUBTLETIES

1. Excerpt from Antonio Machado, from *Proverbs and Tiny Songs*, in Robert Bly (Ed.), *The Soul is Here for its Own Joy*. Ecco Press: Hopewell, NJ, 1995.

2. Excerpt from Chana Bloch, "Firewood," in *The Past Keeps Changing*. Riverdale-on-Hudson, NY: The Sheep Meadow Press, 1992.

3. Excerpt from D.H.Lawrence, "Shadows," in *Last Poems*. New York: Viking, 1932.

CHAPTER 7. PENTIMENTO

1. In one of her most popular books, *Addiction to Perfection*, Marion described how women tried to make themselves into ideals and were killing themselves doing it, through bulimia and hating their bodies.

CHAPTER 9. OPENING TO THE QUESTIONS

1. Peter Kingsley, *In the Dark Places of Wisdom*. Inverness.CA: The Golden Sufi Center, 1999. P. 67.

2. Naomi Newman in collaboration with Martha Boesing, *Snake Talk: Urgent Messages from God the Mother*. A Travelling Jewish Theater, San Francisco, 1986.

3. I am grateful to Rabbi Jonathan Omer-man who told the story about a Wise Rebbe and a man who needed answers in 1989 in Del Mar, California. I have kept the core of the story but changed or elaborated details.

4. A.H. Almaas is the founder of the Diamond Approach to Spiritual Development®. His many books are listed at www.ridhwan.org. For a much fuller treatment of questions and the practice of open-ended inquiry, see *Spacecruiser Inquiry:True Guidance for the Inner Journey.* Boston, MA: Shambhala, 2006).

5. Kingsley, p 67.

6. These comments were first described in Ray & Anderson, 2001.

7. Ray & Anderson, ibid. Ch. 4.

8. Mary Daly, *Gyn/ecology.* Boston: Beacon Press, 1978. p 386-7.

PART IV. RIPENESS

1. A.S. J. Tessimond, *Collected Poems.* Highgreen, England: Bloodaxe Books, 2010.

CHAPTER 10. BECOMING AN ELDER

1. from Barbara Mowat's introduction to Helen M. Luke's *Old Age.* New York: Parabola, 1987. p x. The original quote has a mixture of Luke and Mowat with a number of quotation marks which I've found too distracting for the purposes of an epigraph but will include here: *For those who embrace "the gifts reserved for age"...old age becomes freedom, becomes the dance" into which we may enter...if we have passed through "the purging flame of integration"of these strange gifts.*
    The words enclosed in quotes are Luke's; the others are Mowat's.

2. Luke, op cit. Her phrase "the gifts reserved for age" is from T.S. Eliot's indelible line 131 in "Little Gidding." From a passage, by the way, that Harold Bloom names "purga-

torial," in *Till I End My Song*.

3. Diane Wolkstein and Samuel Noah Kramer, *Inanna*. Harper & Row: New York, 1983. Pp. 58-60.

4. Recounted originally by the Caribou Eskimo, Igjugarjuk, to the scholar and explorer Knud Rasmussen in the 1920's this quote is taken from Richard Tarnas, "The Great Initiation," *Noetic Sciences Review*, no.47, 1988. P. 57.

5. This is described in more detail in Ray & Anderson, Chapter 9.

6. "dark places of wisdom" is Peter Kingsley's term from his book on Parmenides, by the same name. op cit.

7. The Stanford psychologist Laura Carstensen (op cit) and her associates have done two decades of research showing how endings that have great meaning to us bring a sense of poignancy. One simultaneously feels the sweetness of what is ending, and pain or sorrow that it will be gone. This sweet sorrow brings tenderness, gratitude and a recognition of the preciousness of the present moment. We are especially aware of this with the nearness of death but it is true for meaningful endings of all kinds, for people of all ages from teenagers to elders. See also Maurice Sendak's comments that I cite in Chapter 11.

CHAPTER 11. THE PRESENCE OF ELDERS

1. Sandy Scull's poetry is in his *Reaching Across*. Forest Knolls, CA:Croatan Press, 2006. It is also in Maxine Hong Kingston (Ed), *Veterans of War, Veterans of Peace*. Kihei, Hawai'i: Koa Books, 2006.

2. But see A.H. Almaas, *The Unfolding Now: Realizing Your True Nature through the Practice of Presence*. Shambhala: Boston, 2008.

3. Anne Scott describes this time in *Women, Wisdom & Dreams*. Freestone, CA: Nicasio Press, 2008. P. 127.

4. Brenda Ueland, "Tell Me More." *Utne Reader*, November/

December, 1992. Pp 104-105. See also her *Strength to Your Sword Arm: Selected Writings*. Duluth,MN: Holy Cow! Press, 1992.

5. Ellen Bass, op cit.
6. September 2011 NPR *Fresh Air* interview with Terry Gross. See also http://youtube/TH2OaaktJrw, *An Illustrated Talk With Maurice Sendak (Drawings by Christoph Niemann)*.
7. Anthropologist Mary Catherine Bateson calls this period the age of active wisdom. And again, there are multiple names for something that is just showing up on our cultural radar: Adulthood II, the Young Old, the Third Chapter, the Third Age. "Many are grandparents but are like much younger adults," Bateson says. "And for the first time in history, there are large numbers of great-grandparents who look and act somewhat like grandparents used to." Bateson, op cit., p. 13.
8. William H. Thomas, *What Are Old People For?* Acton, MA: VanderWyk & Burnham, 2009. P.199.

CHAPTER 12. ANCESTORS
1. Roxanne Lanier, *The Islands are Asking*. San Francisco: Skimming Stone Press, 1995.

CHAPTER 13. LESSONS FROM THE HARVEST
1. Elizabeth Hanna, a researcher at the Australian National University in Canberra, in "Record Heat Fuels Widespread Fires in Australia." *The Sydney Morning Herald*, January 10, 2013.
2. "Stanley McChrystal: Gun Control Requires 'Serious Action.'" Luke Johnson. *The Huffington Post*. 01/08/2013.
3. Fred Polak, *The Image of the Future*. Trans. Elise Boulding. Elsevier Scientific Pub. Co., 1973. This book is out of print but is available in pdf from Google Books.
4. See Ray & Anderson, op cit. and Paul H. Ray, *The Emerging Planetary Wisdom Culture*. San Francisco: Berrett-Koehler.

Forthcoming.; see also Clay Shirky on how human generosity, new media and technology are transforming us from consumers to collaborators, harnessing the vast amounts of free-floating human potential to build on humanity's treasure trove of knowledge and bring about social change. See his Ted talk at http://youtu.be/qu7ZpWecIS8.

Creating Elders Circles

It can be so helpful, in this season of ripening, to be in a circle of elders. In Chapter 5 particularly, you can see how sticky and strong are Mother Culture's windings, keeping us held in a weave of beliefs and assumptions and out-dated certainties about what it means to grow old. As I hope you know at this point, stepping out of that web is not easy to do all by yourself. But if you can create or join a circle of peers who are respectful of each other, and want to look at their actual experience, question it and delve into the deep truth that keeps unfolding and revealing itself—well, you'll be in good company. And if you can laugh when something's funny and let yourself be tender when something's sensitive and profound, your circle can become a true holding environment for birthing mature elders.

Creating a circle is as easy as inviting two friends to invite two friends—people with enough maturity to want to delve into the deep questions of the inner experience of aging, and enough generosity that you'd be willing to explore your genuine experience in their presence, and that in fact, you would want to share with them and listen to their experience. And creating a circle takes kindness, and courage, and a willingness to be honest with yourself.

If you do not have experience with circles, you will probably find it helpful to read one or two of the references I list below. Even if you have been in a number of circles and groups, these references may give you some good ideas for a new circle. For now, I'll describe a few guidelines that you might like to use.

Some Circle Guidelines

~*How Do You Get Started?* Like anything that addresses a soul-level process, starting a circle starts, I think, with a longing or yearning to be in the company of others who share your intention. There's no point in creating a circle merely because you think you should. Wait to see if you have the heart and will for this kind of creative endeavor. If not, maybe a circle is not a good form for you. It might be far better to meet with one or two good friends and develop a regular meeting time to explore and reflect together. And if that does not appeal to you, perhaps you'd rather journal or take walks or paint or dance or anything your heart desires that gives you a space for the unfolding of your own ripening process.

There is absolutely no right way to create the time and space for your explorations. What you want and need may evolve many times. And at this point, you may have no interest or time to explore anything about growing old and that's just how it is!

~Who Will Come? Start with a group at work or your church or synagogue, with yoga friends or people who have coffee together and run the idea by to see who would like to explore it further. Or invite a friend who invites a friend and let it go around like that. Or just invite whoever strikes your fancy to your home for a drink or dinner. Or start a book discussion group around some of the resources listed here and see if a lively engagement develops.

~What Will the Circle Do? The first way to contemplate this question is to know that a circle has a center. What do you want at the heart of your elders' circle? Try this, if you like, as an early question to people who are considering creating the circle. Some will want silence with a meditative or prayerful core; others will want an open question; or a sense of service; or conscious development. If you let the question circle and circle again, and listen with care to each person, feeling the movement and changes, you'll come to what is worth your precious time. Is there some agreement, or perhaps only some people agree and they can form the circle.

And next you can explore what intrigues or calls to you. This can be a time when you read some books and see some films and look at YouTube and whatever other resources appeal to you. Don't rush. Let this choosing and shaping be fun. You don't have to set anything in stone. How dull that would be! Look at some of the references I list below for ideas on how to play with this process.

~When and Where will the Circle Meet? It helps to have a sense of enclosure, of being pleasantly free from intrusions and comfortable. It's very nice to be able to have tea or candles or music when you want it but that isn't necessary. I've been meeting with one circle for about five years in a sort of grungy rented living room, but it's centrally located and that means a lot to everyone. So you want to find your priorities in choosing your space.

Another circle I meet with is a phone conference scattered along the Atlantic seaboard from Maine to Virginia with one person from Ohio too. We've been meeting every two months for the past year and it seems to be working for us. I hope we can meet in person once a year, but for now, there is a sense of trust and great depth. Sometimes, when no one sees your face, you feel free to say true things more easily.

I know of circles that meet once a year at a retreat center, others that gather for two hours twice a month. There are no rules at all. As the poet Antonio Machado said, you find your way by walking.

The one thing you want to be sure of: that there is enough time for you to feel relaxed about sharing and exploring. Generally, about 6-10 people is a good number for that.

For More Help with Creating and Nurturing Circles
- My website offers a number of resources for creating Elders' Circles: www.SherryRuthAnderson.com.
- Jalaja Bonheim's Institute for Circlework teaches courses

for women and men on the use of circles for healing across many different kinds of boundaries. *www.instituteforcirclework.org*

- Jean Shinoda Bolen's *The Millionth Circle* (Conari Press, 1999) was written primarily for women's circles but has wise advice for all circles. I especially like her chapter on "A Circle in Trouble."
- Charles Garfield, Cindy Spring and Sedonia Cahill give foundational principles for creating resilient circles and building community in their *Wisdom Circles* (Hyperion, 1998).
- Christina Baldwin's *Calling the Circle* (Bantam Books, 1994) has an abundance of creative ideas that you can try out and shape for your own purposes.
- And while not explicitly about circles, *Coming Back to Life: Practices to Reconnect our Lives, Our World* (New Society, 1998) by Joanna Macy and MollyYoung Brown is a treasure chest of questions and practices that are well suited to elders' explorations.

Questions for Discussion and Reflection

Prologue: Is There a Map? Have you wanted a map for growing old, or been asked to give one? What do you think about there being a need for something—a map, true stories, news—for the years ahead of you? If people in their thirties and forties feel there is nothing of value ahead in their sixties and older, will they keep looking back, trying to be who they were and not who they could become? Have you ever felt a longing for elders? For discussion: What do you think about there being a new time now—an extra thirty years of life in which to mature? Does it make you wonder what these extra years could be for?

Part I. Time to Ripen

Chapter 1. A Season of Ripening. Our species has entered this season now—a time when we have a never-before chance to grow up beyond what most of us have barely imagined. Have you thought about this? When you hear about the distinction between growing old and actually maturing, ripening, what kinds of images and memories come up for you? Is this a distinction you've made yourself? What comes up for you if you contemplate full maturity as one of the great human accomplishments? Are you hearing or feeling as sense of invitation to be an elder?

Chapter 2. Old age is boring. Do you feel intrigued by what it's like to be maturing now, or does the whole topic bore you? (Or both!) What impressions about growing old do you have from your childhood? From adolescence? In your twenties and thirties? What are your impressions now?

If you're in a circle or with friends, you can use a repeating question format (described in the previous section) to ask: *Tell me a lie about growing old*. If you do this in a circle, let the first person ask the person to their left this question and go around the circle about 3 times, sending the question around. If you are with a friend, the first person asks the question and says thank you when it is answered, then repeats the question again. So the same person asks the question for 10 or 15 minutes and then the partners change roles.

If you would like to do this alone, simply write the question at the top of a page. Ask it and write your answer. Then ask yourself again and continue for about 10-15 minutes as you wish.

At the end of working with the question, it's good to sit quietly for a few minutes and rest. Then if you like, work with another question like: *Tell me something you know to be true about growing old.*

With these questions and others below, just say what comes to you, including "I don't know." Your partner thanks you and asks the question again. This lets you delve deeper, opening to what is below the conscious mind, discovering how it is to let the questions unfold your experience.

After working with a question or two, and taking time for some silence, let there be a free time for discussion and reflection. It's usually quite interesting to include in this discussion how each person was affected by asking and responding to the particular questions.

Part II. Clearing Obstacles. Explore your response to Jung's observation: *We cannot live the afternoon of life according to the program of life's morning; for what was great in the morning will be little at evening, and what in the morning was true will at evening have become a lie.*

Chapter 3. We Are Already Naked. What is your relationship to your own death? Does it feel real to you, and near, or more distant? How does it affect your relationships? How you choose to spend your time? What you value? Do you talk about it to anyone? How do you distract yourself from this? Do you have experiences that seem untranslatable or unsayable now?

A repeating question to explore: *Tell me what death means to you now.*

After this, take 10 minutes or more to sit in silence or the write in a journal. If you wish, follow this with time for reflection and sharing. Be very respectful of each person's preferences here. Some may not want to speak. Discuss how you want to do this.

Chapter 4. When your Mind is not Clouded. Do you ever feel like just going back to the way things were before? Take some time to imagine being one of your grandparents and speak from their point of view for about 5 minutes about: how you feel about your body; what your hopes are for your grandchildren; what you value in this life. If you're in a circle or with a partner, let each person do this and then reflect together on what this perspective brings up for you.

Repeating questions to explore:

(1) *Tell me a way you are pessimistic about growing old.*
(2) *Tell me a way you are optimistic about growing old.*
(3) *Tell me something you don't know about growing old.*

As before, take some time for silence, and then some free time for discussion and reflection. Again, you may want to include how each person was affected by the process.

Chapter 5. Escaping Mother Culture's Web. Can you hear Mother Culture humming her story about what it means to grow old? What do you hear these days, and see, about the weaving of this story? Are you tempted to ask people around you? How can you believe this stuff? Have you done it? Can you spot how you have stepped into your place in age roles over the years? How you fit others into these roles? How does this affect your relationships? What happens when you step outside the roles?

Repeating questions: (1) *Tell me what it is like to be the age you are now.*

And after that, try (2): *Tell me a way you are a person of no age.*

As before, take time for silence and sharing with your circle or friends.

Chapter 6. Secrets & Subtleties. This is a good place to share some of the different kinds of stories that come into the weave of aging: *the ones that make you laugh; the hard ones we tend to hide; and the ones we may have no words for—not so much secrets but subtleties.* If you're sharing these in a circle, it will be essential to remember to be respectful and sensitive to the latter two. This may be especially true for the subtle experiences. When people share about these, it is vulnerable and can be quite beautiful and moving. One way to keep this quality of sharing at a distance is to joke about it. If that happens, see if you can name what is happening. If you ask what about this kind of sharing makes someone uncomfortable, the sharing is likely to become more genuine and a new level of trust can develop in the circle or between the friends who are exploring together.

Chapter 7. Pentimento. Explore your response to this quote from poet Chana Bloch: *There's no way to change/ without touching/ the space at the center of everything.* Do you find yourself saying at times, "Maybe I'm just getting old?" When do you say that? What are you assuming about your experience at that point? Do you end up dismissing something that might actually be new, or unknown? How do you feel about experiences that are untranslatable or mysterious as you age, the kind that don't fit conventional ideas and expectations?

Part III. Cultivation
Chapter 8. Disturbing the Furies. Are there ways you have been

naive or just mistaken about what it means to grow old? What do you feel now as you look back on those times? How is it to see younger people making assumptions about what you experience now?

Chapter 9. Opening to the Questions. How do you feel about loving your own questions? How do you feel about asking questions? How were your questions received when you were a child? When you were a teenager? What is your attitude when you ask a question? Did the story of Rose and Wise Elder have any resonance with your own experience? Have you traded your precious questions for somebody else's answers? Discuss what the following quote brings up for you: *"It's as if we're each in our own cocoon, unable to see what is unfolding. We're in the process of birthing the membrane that holds the new elder. We're going through for the first time, making our way toward a new way of aging most of us have never seen before."*

Part IV. Ripeness. What does "ripening" mean to you at this point? Does it have any relevance to your life now? How do you feel about letting the clocks stop?

Chapter 10. Becoming an Elder. How do you feel about being an elder? What does the word mean to you? Have you wanted to be an elder? Avoided it? What do you think of the perspective that says the "hard stuff" of life is what transforms and matures us, if we can be present for it? Have you had an experience of coming close to death yourself? How has it affected you? How do you feel about the endings that are near or have already occurred in your life? What is opened in you, or shut down, by these times?

Chapter 11. The Presence of Elders. Discuss this idea: *Many times, the fruit of a life deeply lived is almost invisible, and elders* *themselves may not recognize it. But it has great value nevertheless. It is the gift of presence.* Have you had experiences with elders who are present in a community or as friends? Have you found your own presence making a difference to others? What words do you use for these kinds of experiences? What do you find supports the development of presence in yourself? In your community or work or family? Have you personally felt the sense of generosity that comes with aging? Have you also felt the other side, a need to hold tight to what you have? Take time to discuss both sides in your circle or with friends.

Chapter 12. Ancestors. Discuss poet Roxanne Lanier's view and its relevance—or not—for your sense of being connected beyond those you know: *I am part of a network of events/that have occurred in the lives of many people, some of whom are unknown to me... To be aware of this is to carry their love within my heart/and to live in a spirit of gratitude.* What do you think of the belief that elders are bridges, links of continuity between the ancestors and the children yet to come? What do you feel about your relationship to your own ancestors or those who have preceded you? Has your view changed over the years?

Part V. Harvest
Chapter 13. Lessons from the Harvest. From where you are now, how do you feel about growing old? What do you see about this time we are in where there is "an evolutionary jump in elders who can become mature and a need for mature wisdom that grows more urgent by the day?" How do you feel about changing the future of aging? What is it like to contemplate the humanity that has been developing in you all these years? What do you love that you want to stand for?

Some final repeating questions to explore in a circle or with a friend or two (as described in the Chapter 2 section above): (1) *Tell me something real that has been developing in you.* (2) *Tell me something you love.* (3) *Tell me a way you are an elder.*

As before, take time for silence and then for sharing how it was to explore these questions and whatever else you wish.

Resources

These are selected favorites of mine for your enjoyment. The resources that I used for this book are fully described in the End Notes. See my website for further resources: www.SherryRuthAnderson.com.

Being an Elder: The Inside Story

Elizabeth Bugental, *AgeSong: Meditations for Our Later Years.* San Francisco: Elders Academy Press, 2005.

Carolyn G. Heilbrun, *The Last Gift of Time: Life Beyond Sixty.* New York: Ballentine, 1997.

Helen Luke, *Old Age.* New York: Parabola, 1987.

Susan Moon, *This is Getting Old.* Boston: Shambhala, 2010.

Barbara Myerhoff, *Stories as Equipment for Living.* Ann Arbor, MI:University of Michigan Press, 2007.

Internet Links

Sherry Ruth Anderson on Aging as Awakening. YouTube link: http://youtu.be/yKQzyvBtsIQ

Dr. Jean Shinoda Bolen shares the importance of holding the 5th Women's World Conference (5WWC) and why every women needs to stand behind the event. She also shares tips and tools to find your assignment in life. One way of being an elder: as an activist. Very inspiring. YouTube link: http://youtu.be/d-GeLMX4Vf0

Psychologist James Hillman On The Legacy Of Aging. Jungian psychologist James Hillman is the author of "The Force of Character and The Lasting Life". Hillman explains why he believes that a person's true character only emerges in old age. I like his views on "waking up to the night." YouTube link: .http://youtu.be/ja02wofquG8

Zen Teacher Lewis Richmond on Enjoying Your Old Age.

YouTube link: http://youtu.be/Mo6_BGvcQWg

Marion Woodman: Dancing in the Flames - 'Two Marions.' A wise elder on including the opposites. YouTube link: http://youtu.be/BA251K83RxA

Being an Elder: The Research

Mary Catherine Bateson, *Composing A Future Life: The Age of Active Wisdom*. New York: Knopf, 2010.

Laura L. Carstensen, *A Long Bright Future*. New York: Broadway Books, 2009.

Gene D. Cohen, *The Mature Mind: The Positive Power of the Aging Brain*. New York: Basic Books, 2005.

Elkhonon Goldberg, *The Wisdom Paradox*. New York: Gotham, 2005.

Sherwin B. Nuland, *The Art of Aging*. New York: Random House, 2007.

William H. Thomas, What are Old People For? Acton, MA: Vanderwyk & Burnham, 2004.

Lars Tornstam, *Gerotranscendence: A Developmental Theory of Positive Aging*. New York: Springer, 2005.

Being Present to the Unfolding Mystery

A.H.Almaas, *Diamond Heart Book Five: Inexhaustible Mystery*. Boston: Shambhala, 2011.

—, *The Unfolding Now*. Boston: Shambhala, 2008.

Paula D'Arcy, *Waking Up to This Day*. Maryknoll, NY: Orbis Books, 2009.

Peter Kingsely, In the Dark Places of Wisdom. Inverness, CA: The Golden Sufi Center, 1999.

Eckhart Tolle, *The Power of Now*. Novato, CA: New World Library, 1999.

A Small Selection of the Irresistible

Ellen Bass. *The Human Line*. Port Townsend, WA: Copper Canyon

Press, 2007.

Harold Bloom (Ed.), *Till I End My Song: A Gathering of Last Poems*. New York: Harper-Collins, 2010.

Roger Housden, *Ten Poems to Say Goodbye*. New York: Harmony, 2012.

Jane Hirshfield, *Come, Thief*. New York: Borzoi, 2011.

W.S. Merwin, *The Shadow of Sirius*. Port Townsend, WA: Copper Canyon Press, 2009.

Henry Miller, *To Paint is to Love Again*. Alhambra, CA: Cambria Books, 1960.

Acknowledgements

I want to offer special thanks to Vanda Marlow for being the muse who handed me the assignment with my name on it and cheered me on through all of the writing, and to my dear friend and writing colleague Marcia Wakeland, who helped me stay in alignment with the book's purpose. The contributions of Jim Thomas and Ann Kerr Linden are threaded throughout this book and helped significantly to shape my thinking.

The early support of my writing group—Lama Palden Alioto, Vanda Marlow and Jennifer Welwood—was invaluable in reminding me to tell my own story and speak in my own voice. David Kundt, Janine Canan and Rosanne Annoni were especially skillful and generous in their comments. Darryl Paffenroth, Fred Mitouer and Gail Horvath and Rabbi Spike Anderson and Marita Gringaus Anderson were true friends in their support and encouragement.

I want particularly to thank the artist Heather Preston for the great gift of her cover art to portray the harvest season, and winemaker Jacques Schlumberger for his generosity in revealing the secrets of the crush.

I've been blessed with the kindness and skill of many readers and I particularly want to thank Adeline van Waning, Barbara Zilber, David Silverstein, Gay Gaer Luce, Jeanine Mamary Ball, Joan Bieder, Karen Dega, Meredith Beam, Patricia Hopkins, Roger Housden, Sara Harris, Sylvia Boorstien and Thomas Weinberg.

The great and continuing inspiration for this writing has been the elders I have been privileged to learn from over the years, in seminars at the Ridhwan Center and Spirit Rock Meditation Center and Wisdom University and retreats in many locations.

Finally, I am grateful beyond words to my beloved Paul for being a true partner in every way in bringing this book to its final form.

Permissions